Curing the Crisis

Michael D. Reagan

Curing the Crisis
Options for America's Health Care

WESTVIEW PRESS
Boulder • San Francisco • Oxford

Copyright © 1992 by Westview Press, Inc.

Published in 1992 in the United States of America by Westview Press, Inc., 5500 Central Avenue, Boulder, Colorado 80301-2847, and in the United Kingdom by Westview Press, 36 Lonsdale Road, Summertown, Oxford OX2 7EW

Library of Congress Cataloging-in-Publication Data
Reagan, Michael D.
  Curing the crisis : options for America's health care / Michael D. Reagan.
    p. cm.
  Includes bibliographical references and index.
  ISBN 0-8133-8179-7 (cloth).—ISBN 0-8133-8180-0 (pb)
  1. Medical care, Cost of—United States.   2. Medical policy—
United States.   3. Insurance, Health—United States.   I. Title.
[DNLM: 1. Delivery of Health Care—economics—United States.
2. Health Care Costs—United States.   3. Insurance, Health—
economics—United States.   W 84 AA1 R225c]
RA410.53.R38   1992
362.1'0973—dc20
DNLM/DLC   92-15706
for Library of Congress   CIP

Printed and bound in the United States of America

⊗ The paper used in this publication meets the requirements
    of the American National Standard for Permanence of Paper
    for Printed Library Materials Z39.48-1984.

10   9   8   7   6   5   4   3

For Bob

Contents

PART ONE   A Snapshot of Health Care Delivery Today

1   Perspectives and Perceptions   3

2   The Changing Profile of U.S. Health Care   13

    The System Today, 13
    Box: HMOs, PPOs, EPOs, and Hybrids, 18
    Reversing Incentives: Don't Do More, Do Less, 23
    How the System Developed: A Hospital-Oriented
       Sketch, 27
    Cross Subsidies and the Loss of Community, 34

PART TWO   Understanding the Problems

3   What Are the Problems?   39

    Access: Who Has It? Who Does Not? 39
    Box: Lack of Care from Coast to Coast, 44
    Health Care Leads the Inflation Index, 50
    We, the People, Expect Better Health Care, 54

4   What's Causing the Problems?   57

    How a Market System Works: No Insurance,
       No Access, 57
    Why Do Costs Rise So Much, So Fast? 64
    High-Tech: Its Use, Abuse, and Costs, 67
    Payment Perversities and Moral Hazard, 72
    The Changing Picture of Incentives, 77
    Where Are the Levers of Budgetary Control? 78

PART THREE   What Are the Options?

5   How Do We Get Coverage for Everyone?   83

    The Red Herring of Socialized Medicine, 83
    What Is the Range of Options? 85

The NHS Concept and Its British Version, 86
NHI: The Canadian Case, 88
NHI: A Physician-sponsored Plan, 91
UHI: The German Version, 94
UHI: The Play-or-Pay Approach, 97
The Mandate Approach, 103
Making Private Insurance More Accessible, 106
The Privatized, Individualized Approach, 108

6   Cutting Costs: Piecemeal Approaches   111

     The Economic Model—and Its Dangers, 114
     The Medical Model: Making the Practice of Medicine
          More (Cost) Effective, 126

7   Cutting Costs: Overall Approaches   139

     Patients and Doctors, 139
     Box: Improving the Doctor-Patient Relationship, 141
     Capacity Constraints and Health Care Rationing, 147

PART FOUR   Components of an Achievable Better System

8   Elements for an Optimal Health Care Plan   163

     The Givens of Reform, 163
     Box: How Much Change Is the Public Ready For? 164
     Elements of an Optimal Plan, 167
     Box: Preserving Pluralism, 173
     Encourage Professionalism, Discourage
          Micromanagement, 174
     Plan A, Plan B, 175
     Time for Action, Time for Leadership, 176

Notes   177
List of Acronyms and Glossary   181
Suggested Readings   187
About the Book and Author   189
Index   191

Part One

A Snapshot of Health Care Delivery Today

1
Perspectives and Perceptions

How is the American health care system doing? The answer depends on where we put the stethoscope and who is doing the diagnosis.

Looking at the results of distributing health services largely on a price basis (i.e., if you have the dollars, you can get the service), international health economist Uwe Reinhardt is highly critical. "Uniquely in the industrialized world," he writes, "American health care exhibits opulent splendor and shocking deprivation side by side."[1]

With a different lens, Dr. Carl Weber, a surgeon in private practice, points out with pride that the United States cut the death rates for cardiovascular disease 10 percent and the rate for cerebrovascular disease 19 percent from 1980 to 1985; England's improvement was 3 and 5 percent, respectively. He points also to the queuing (waiting lists) for operations in England—patients wait 18 months on average for a hip replacement—and his *New York Times* (May 30, 1990) commentary is titled "In Health Care, U.S. Is Best."

"Where we sit is where we stand" is a relevant aphorism. Our perceptions derive from the pictures already in our heads as well as from objective facts, and the health care system is so large and so complex that there are many, many perspectives. The result is a bewildering and often paradoxical range of opinions. Depending on what you happen to read, you may gain very different pictures of how well our health care needs are being served. And the reader's sense of what needs to be done will also depend on where she or he sits: If a person has top-drawer insurance coverage paid for by an employer, the system is going to appear a lot healthier than it appears to someone working for a small firm that does not provide health benefits or to someone who has a low income but one not quite low enough to qualify for Medicaid (the jointly financed federal-state health program for some of the poor).

A seemingly endless list can be made of interested parties in health care and health care policy: doctors, patients, nurses, hospital administrators, prosthesis manufacturers, insurance companies, physical therapists, utilization reviewers, public health officers, medical school deans, large and small employers, state governments, managed-care consulting firms, the agency that administers Medicare and Medicaid, the National Institutes of Health, lobbyists for the Alzheimer's Association, pharmaceutical manufacturers—and literally hundreds of health-related organizations ranging from the American Academy of Podiatric Sports Medicine and the American Medical Association through the Group Health Association of America and the National Hemophilia Foundation to the U.S. Department of Health and Human Services. All of these groups evaluate differently the strengths and weaknesses of our medical capabilities and our ways of distributing services to patients.

Here, to illustrate, are the responses you might get if you were to ask some participants in the essential, exciting, and expensive adventure of U.S. health care how well they think we are doing.

- A corporate leader or employee-benefits manager might tell you:

Our employees have a good thing going in their health benefits. Too good, in fact. Because the company has been paying all or most of the bills, workers haven't had to think about costs, so they've overused doctors and hospitals.

But the costs of health care have a decidedly unhealthy effect on our balance sheet. Our sales may go up 8 percent this year, but our employee health insurance premium will probably go up 15–20 percent. In 1965, corporate health care spending consumed 4–8 cents per dollar of profit; by 1990, it was 25–50 percent. And business's share of the health care spending burden has risen from 17 percent in 1965 to 30 percent in 1989.

Our workers are losing out, too—more than they know. A report from the Employee Benefit Research Institute shows that direct wage and salary compensation by corporations, per employee, rose only 1 percent over the 1970–1989 period (measured in constant 1989 dollars), but health benefits went up *163* percent.

My company suffers because our overseas competitors don't shoulder the same burden. We've got to cut costs, or accept nationalized health care.

- The U.S. Congress, through its collective actions, is saying:

Medicare is a fine service for our elderly citizens. But for too long we let the hospitals and the doctors dictate the terms of their participation in this taxpayer-funded program, so charges rose too high. The taxpayers' Medicare bill rose from $5.1 billion in 1968 to $110 billion in 1990. We've already taken steps to slow down hospital costs; now we're beginning to impose new constraints on physician charges, too.

The medical care is great, but the cost is too high. The most effective remedy we have found is to squeeze the incomes of the providers (the hospitals, doctors, and other health professionals) supplying the services. We think there is enough slack in the system so that we can do this without hurting either their willingness to meet the health needs of the elderly, or the quality of care provided.

- A medical researcher or university health center specialist might say:

We're doing fine. Look at the practical results of research since the 1950s: amniocentesis, polio vaccines, coronary bypass surgery, specialized intensive care units, laser treatments, organ transplants, hip and knee replacements, the development of noninvasive imaging machines, and an ever-proliferating catalog of prescription medications. We even have a technique—laparoscopic cholecystectomy—that uses a television camera inside the body to guide a surgeon in removing the gallbladder through a tiny incision. The patient is home in a day rather than a week and is able to resume normal activities in a week's time rather than the six weeks customary after traditional surgery that cuts into abdominal wall muscles.

Medicine has already been revolutionized by recent research, but that's only the beginning. Look at what's coming along: a temporary artificial lung that will be simpler, less costly, and safer than existing mechanical ventilators; growth hormone supplements that actually slow the effects of aging; and—the most exciting frontier—disease treatment through gene modification. Just increase the National Institutes of Health budget (and its grants to university medical researchers), and we'll have more and better miracles to report in future years. One now in development, for example, is electrotransport of medications, in which genetically engineered drugs may be propelled through the skin by a small electrical current.

- Some practitioners of the "dismal science" (economics) look at the financial incentives pattern of providing health care and say:

We're probably spending too much on health care relative to other needs that the same funds could meet. In the third-party payment system the doctor, the first party, treats the patient, the second party, and the insurance company or employer or government program, the third party, pays for the transaction. In the fee-for-service billing system, a fee is charged for each separate service rendered. By combining these systems, we encourage over-utilization of medical care. A system that sets payment limits in advance of treatment—called prospective payment, or PPS—makes providers compete and makes patients pay enough of the charges to think twice before asking for unnecessary services. That's the way to handle this resource allocation problem in a free market economy.

• As usual, however, economists are split into rival camps, and some of those most knowledgeable about health care matters argue this way:

The Canadian and British health systems—though quite different from one another in crucial ways—both largely avoid imposing cost-sharing charges on patients yet have lower costs per capita and as a share of gross national product than we have in the United States.

As for competition, we were obsessed with it during the 1980s, but it has not noticeably reduced the rate of cost increase. What it clearly has done, however, is to cause disruption and skewing of services. Now, in the 1990s, competition is propelling an effort by insurers to avoid clients who have needed medical care in the past or who possess "indicators" of potentially heavy use in the future.

• An advocate for the health care needs of the uninsured might re-spond to the more hopeful evaluations in this manner:

Despite spending almost three-quarters of a trillion dollars a year on health care, 31–37 million Americans currently lack health insurance. (Estimates vary widely, with 35.7 million in 1990 probably the closest to a consensus figure—at least until the 1991 recession added perhaps a million more who lost their insurance when they lost their jobs.) We think of the uninsured as the poor and unemployed, assuming that the employed all enjoy mid-dle-class employee-benefit health insurance. But that's a myth. Eighty-four percent of the uninsured live in families where the head of the family is em-ployed. Health coverage in the United States has actually shrunk in the pro-portion of the population covered in recent years, falling from about 88 per-cent in 1978 to 84 percent in 1989—and each percentage point is 2.5 million people. Medical science may be doing fine, but the system of deliv-ering medical care to the people isn't working.

- And a state Medicaid administrator might add:

> Some may suppose that the unemployed poor have an advantage here—that Medicaid takes care of them. Everyone speaks of this program as if it covered all poor persons—but it doesn't even come close. First, the patient can't just be poor. She—less often he—has to fit a specific category, such as being a single parent with a dependent child and eligible for welfare. And most state legislatures have set the income limit for welfare so low that a majority of those who are poor by federal poverty standards are, incredibly, too "well off" by state eligibility guidelines to be eligible for help.

The complex reality behind this range of perceptions is even reflected in pronouncements from the citadel of organized medicine, the American Medical Association (AMA). The AMA's Executive Director, Dr. James S. Todd, writes of contradictory elements in U.S. health care. He asserts that our system "at its best is universally acknowledged to be the best in the world," yet concedes that "enormous problems . . . exist." After enthusing about "the can-do spirit that has fostered what is best in American medicine—the breakthrough research, technological advances, and widespread availability of life-enhancing procedures," he turns around and calls for a "greater sense of restraint" in availing ourselves of these marvels, because "we can no longer do everything for everybody just because it is possible."[2]

- The perspective of an individual physician, one whose practice has spanned the pre- and post–Medicare/Medicaid eras, might run like this:

> Once I could be a true professional—a person whose medical judgment went unchallenged by patient or payer. As a solo practitioner, I took patient histories myself, performed simple tests, made diagnoses, prescribed medicines, and decided when and for how long my patient might need hospitalization. My fees were my own business, higher for my well-off patients so that I could afford to treat the indigent according to my conscience. There was little second-guessing—now called "utilization review"—and government generally did not intrude between me and my patients.
>
> Now an increasing proportion of my younger colleagues practice in health maintenance organizations, or HMOs, and other group arrangements. They have better hours and better equipment—possible because the expense is shared within the group—and the range of medicines, devices,

and procedures they can draw upon is a wondrous thing, enabling them to "recondition" human bodies in ways not dreamed of when I began practice. But they pay a price.

They have lost some of their professional autonomy, subject as they are to a variety of new constraints: the protocols and even productivity standards set by their employers if they are part of an HMO staff; the urgings of hospital administrators, or of insurance clearance personnel, to discharge patients at the earliest possible moment; and the increasing fee constraints of Medicare and other third-party payers, making it harder to continue the amount of charity care they would like to do for the uninsured. Physicians are also encouraged by the malpractice incentive to overdo things in order to avoid lawsuits based on the premise that every single thing possible should be done. Physicians may also overdo in order to avoid questioning of their judgment by the much less submissive patients of today.

Medicine is increasingly practiced in bureaucratic organizations operating in a context that seems to treat the financial health of the institution as equal in status with good patient care. One result of the challenges to professional autonomy: In a 1990 AMA survey, 48 percent of doctors over age 35 said they would not recommend medicine as a career choice to students.

• The chief administrator of a hospital, whether or not he or she is a physician, looks at the situation through a different lens:

The doctors want me to provide them with their "workshop," including the latest equipment and the most experienced nursing staff. Then they want me to just leave them alone to practice as they see fit.

We have a lot of Medicare patients, however, and HCFA (Health Care Financing Administration—the agency within the U.S. Department of Health and Human Services that administers Medicare and Medicaid) no longer reimburses us for whatever costs our attending physicians may incur on our behalf by their orders for tests or for a longer stay for their patients. Instead, Medicare tells us in advance what we will be paid for inpatient treatment of a particular diagnosis—called a DRG, for Diagnostic Related Group—regardless of our costs and bases its allowed charge largely on the number of hospital days usual for that treatment. So we have to "beg and plead and cajole and put a lot of pressure" (in the words of a former hospital administrator)[3] on the doctors to release patients early. And when the patient is sent home before feeling as fully recovered as might have been the case in the old days, we get accused of discharging him "quicker and sicker."

The community at large insists that we keep open our 7-day, 24-hour emergency room—but the community does not provide enough charitable contribution support to cover the costs incurred by the high proportion of uninsured ER patients—the homeless, the kids from motorcycle accidents, the unemployed, and even the employed who couldn't get insurance or who passed up the opportunity, saying "I'll never get sick."

Until recently, we could cross-subsidize our "uncompensated," or charity, care with reimbursements from employer-paid insurance plans that paid our full costs, including a share of indigent patient care. Now the employers are squeezing their insurers and refusing to share the community burden. In fact, they now want us to be a "preferred provider," which means to give them a discount!

The doctors intensely resent our overseeing their modes of practice and our insistence that cost effectiveness has to be a component of quality care today. But the fact is that they'll lose their workshop and the community its essential facility if we in the front office don't keep the bottom line in black ink.

No wonder the turnover rate among hospital chief executives rose sharply in the past decade and may be twice that of chief executive officers (CEOs) generally.

• Quite a different emphasis from that of the providers of acute care emerges in the views of a public health officer, one whose focus is on organized community efforts to prevent disease and to promote good health:

On the plus side, we can point out that overall U.S. life expectancy rose from 47 years in 1900 to 75.2 years in 1990. And infant mortality was reduced by nearly 50 percent between 1960 and 1980. On the minus side, it is appalling that the 1989 figure of 9.7 deaths per 1,000 live births put the U.S. ranking that year behind that for Hong Kong and Singapore. Lack of prenatal care as the major reason becomes understandable when one learns that only .3 percent of our national health expenditures are for health promotion and disease prevention.

From a public health perspective, I must constantly point out to local, state, and federal budget makers that the major health improvements of the past century reflect declining deaths from infectious diseases; we have eradicated smallpox and nearly eliminated polio. And these dramatic changes are more the result of improved sanitation, clean water, better diets, and mass immunization and innoculation programs than of acute treatment of individual illnesses.

I point out to them that three-tenths of 1 percent of the national budget devoted to prevention and health promotion is hardly going to produce equivalent progress in the next generation when the leading causes of death are now related to life-style: preventable accidents, cancer from smoking, fatty-diet-induced heart attacks and strokes, hypertension, and liver disease from alcohol abuse. Our individual behavior and largely preventable environmental hazards, for example, industrial toxics in the air and water, were estimated to lie behind 70 percent of the 10 leading causes of death in a study of 1976 data. So I am frustrated by constantly escalating expenditures on acute care episodes while we largely ignore what can be done to *avoid* the need for treatment in the first place.

True, recent reductions in cigarette and alcohol consumption rates and in the rate of deaths from heart disease provide some room for optimism, but there can be little such optimism about the near-term prospects of a cure for the greatest of all new public health menaces: AIDS.

Finally, I have to point out that we are moving backward in some parts of public health, even as news releases celebrate new transplant procedures and other high-tech innovations. The United States ranks a not-very-respectable seventeenth among nations in vaccinating against common childhood diseases. One example: Because many, many young children were not receiving the "usual" childhood shots, there was a startling resurgence of measles, with 26,500 cases in 1990, up from a low of 1,500 in 1983. Despite some decline in measles cases in 1991—partly because of more aggressive public immunization efforts and partly as a natural result of those who caught the disease becoming immune and no longer being able to spread it—the victory over infectious diseases may be unraveling, though the champagne corks have long since been popped.

I ask, Don't we need to rethink our priorities in the total health care picture?

Finally, what about us, Jane and John Q. Public? How do we see things?

We are running scared, and that is turning health care from a social problem into a political issue. What was once a problem for "them" (the people on welfare eligible for Medicaid; some of the unemployed not eligible for anything) is now being perceived as a problem for "us."

That showed up most dramatically in the 1991 Senate race in Pennsylvania when Senator Harris Wofford (D., Penn.) effectively dramatized his case by emphasizing health insurance worries as the greatest single source of domestic policy concern.

We have been mixed in our responses to pollsters asking about health care, telling them both that the system needs drastic change and that we are satisfied with our own doctors. In 1992, the dissatisfaction has clearly gained the upper hand. And that means we as a nation may at last be ready to give serious consideration to alternative approaches to providing access to health care and to paying for it.

To grapple with the twin crises of availability and cost requires that we move beyond pious statements that everyone should be covered and get down to brass tacks. Do we want employers to provide health insurance for all employees as a matter of law? Are we open to considering a totally tax-supported national health plan like the one in Canada that is so often mentioned? Or do we just want minor tinkering with existing private health insurance, and let the market do what it can, even if that means some people are still left outside the system?

And what about the costs of health care? Does it matter to us that it now consumes over 12 percent of our gross national product (GNP)? If it does matter, how much so? To reduce cost escalation would we be willing to lose free choice of physician? To wait for elective surgeries? To increase the share we pay out-of-pocket beyond what our insurance covers?

These are but a sampling of the kinds of questions that need to be addressed. And to do that, we all need to become familiar with a wide range of facts, figures, and acronymic concepts and organizations.

That's what this book is about—providing information and analysis of our health care situation. We'll look at the problems and their causes and the major types of proposals for ensuring that everyone has coverage and for containing costs. At the end, I'll propose a set of elements that should be included in any major reform legislation. In analyzing the pros and cons of different options, I necessarily depart from a straight "only the facts, ma'am" approach, for all evaluation is done from the analyst's own value perspective. In my case, the value imperative is to see that every American receives health care on the basis of need, not wallet.

2
The Changing Profile of U.S. Health Care

Before the doctor even discusses my symptoms with me, she will note my basic characteristics—male or female, age 6 or 27 or 83, overweight or underweight, pale looking or robust in appearance, and so on—and take a medical history.

Analogously, this chapter profiles the health care system as if it were a patient. To understand its operation today we have to describe both its history and its current organizational and financial structure. Heart transplants and miracle drugs make the headlines, but the less dramatic changes in institutional patterns are equally significant.

These are the orienting questions for this chapter:

- What are the major characteristics of the U.S. health care system today? And how did they get to be what they are?

- What trends are now apparent, and how are these changing the system's crucial characteristics?

- What forces have produced the current trends that make health reform a fundamental policy challenge for the 1990s?

The System Today

The System Is Predominantly Private

U.S. health care is predominantly a *private* matter, financially speaking. Unlike education—a tax-supported service with which it is often compared as a basic need of all citizens—health care is primarily sold in a market transaction by doctors, hospitals, and other private suppliers (generally called "providers"), with private-sector payments accounting for about 58 percent of the $666 billion national health expenditure estimated for 1990. We are the only industrial nation other than South Africa in which the public (government-financed) sector share of health care is less than 60 percent. In the United States, health care is, in fact, a very big business—the nation's third largest industry (after manufacturing and retailing) in employment terms, with 500,000 practicing physicians and millions of nurses and other health care professionals, all utilizing about 5,500 acute care hospitals.

Even for those among the aged and poor whose medical bills are paid out of government funds, the services are generally delivered not by civil servants but by the same private parties serving patients whose payments are made by private employers, insurance companies, or out-of-pocket. The phrase "public-sector health services" derives mostly from who picks up the tab, not who provides the care. (Some small public-sector programs do provide direct services: the Indian Health Service, Community Health Centers, the National Health Service Corps, and many county health department clinics. And of course there is direct provision for health services in the military and in veterans' hospitals.)

As most readers will recognize from their own experience, "private" payment does not mean that health care is typically purchased by individuals for themselves and their families, like buying a car or a TV set. Overwhelmingly, health care "purchases" consist of signing up for largely employer-provided, tax-subsidized, group health insurance. Only 19 percent of private health insurance was not employment-derived in 1988. The insurance, of course, does not reimburse for all medical expenses. Coverage is not complete, especially for medications, and employers increasingly impose cost-sharing requirements on employees.

Health insurance is expensive. Even at the group rates paid by employers it averaged $3,217 in 1990 per employee, or 26 percent of the average firm's net earnings, according to a survey by the consulting firm of A. Foster Higgins. Because individual policies cost substantially more, most families cannot (and some will not) purchase them. For the working-age population, therefore, health insurance is much more a privilege of employment than a right of citizenship.

One further dimension of the private system: It is very much fragmented. Until the end of World War II, Blue Cross was clearly dominant as the nation's health insurer. By 1987, however, there were 1,500 commercial health insurers holding 40 percent of the market; self-insured employers covered 37 percent, and Blue Cross–Blue Shield had 25–27 percent. Almost all observers see this profusion of providers (and many of them offer different plans, to complicate things further) as highly inefficient and substantially influencing the high costs of U.S. health care.

Since 1965, the private system has been largely augmented by Medicare for the 65-and-over population and the disabled and by Medicaid for some of the poor. These are public insurance systems: They pay bills but do not directly provide the services. Although both have substantially aided people with limited incomes to obtain medical care, they leave major gaps unfilled.

If we count both public and private insurance systems, 1988 figures show insurance payment for 87 percent of hospitalization (that does not include nursing homes), 72 percent of physician bills, and about one-third of drug expenditures (an item Medicare does not include). Overall, about three-fourths of all health care bills are picked up by insurance programs of one type or another.

The Bill Payers Are Third Parties

Ours has become a third-party payer system. The physician (Party One) and the patient (Party Two) have until quite recently been somewhat insulated from the crasser facts of health care finance by leaving most of the bill paying to the insuring entity (Party Three). In this respect, our system, although private in the simple sense of being nongovernmental, is indeed more "socialized" than individualized in character. This fundamental dimension of the way we pay for medical care significantly affects the attitudes toward using care on the part of patients, providers, and payers as it interacts with varying incentive systems to be examined later.

Ours is also the only industrial democracy (with the exception once again of South Africa) that has a substantial population without any health insurance at all. Over 35 million Americans are uninsured because our system is employment-based and market-oriented, whereas Canada, the European countries, and Japan all have legislation providing for tax-based and need-oriented health coverage for all citizens. (See Chapter 5.)

The Cost Is the Highest in the World

Perhaps the most astounding aspect of the U.S. health care profile is its lack of cost-effectiveness: Despite leaving millions of people uninsured and having unimpressive life-expectancy and infant-mortality records compared with other nations, we still have the highest-priced system in the world. On a per capita basis we spent $2,566 in 1990; or 12.4 percent of gross domestic product (GDP, or GNP less international earnings). Canada—with the next most expensive system, but one that includes the entire population—spent $1,795 per person in 1990, and Germany spent $1,287. The problem is not just high cost, but that those costs are ever-increasing. Health care inflation has outstripped general inflation for many years and continues to do so. The 1970 to 1990 increase in the consumer price index (CPI) compares with the health increase as follows, using the 1982–1984 average as an index number of 100:

	1970	1990
CPI	38.8	130.7
Health care overall	34	162.8

These figures amount to a 20-year increase of 337 percent in the CPI and 479 percent in health expenditures.

It's easy to see why "cost containment" has become the defining goal of those organizations, be they private corporations or government agencies, that pay the third-party bills.

Challenges to Professional Dominance from All Sides

A closely related dimension—and a very new one—is the ongoing shift in those we can call the dominant players from the professional providers (doctors and hospitals in particular) to the organized "buyers" of health care. Although it would be too much to say that the professional dominance of physicians has become a thing of the past, it has certainly diminished and is under continuing challenge. "Organized medicine" (that is, the AMA and other associations) no longer dictates the economic forms in which medicine can be practiced, as in the days when the AMA considered it unethical for a doctor to be part of a prepaid group practice. But also, the influence of nonmedical personnel extends to the area of medical judgment;

the individual doctor's decisions are sometimes challenged by representatives of both private insurers and Medicare.

This buyer-payer power is developing in paradoxical tandem with what is in some respects an opposite and equally new assertiveness on the part of patients. Because of a generally better-educated population that is also astonishingly (if sometimes faddishly) health conscious, the established doctrine of "informed consent" is being greatly broadened. Patients expect to be told what is wrong with them and to be able to make their own decisions on treatment options rather than have one course of treatment dictated. They are even insisting on telling their doctors when *not* to do anything more to them. Fitting the new prerogatives of patients and payers together is one of today's larger challenges to the medical profession.

An Organizational Revolution in Health Care

The dominant mode of organization for delivering health care services is the same today as it has been for several generations: a solo-practice doctor and a free-standing (that is, not part of a national chain) community hospital. New patterns—collectively referred to as "alternative delivery systems" (ADS)—have emerged in recent years, however, so that a substantial minority of services are now provided by medical groups and chain hospitals, including some for-profit chains. Individual practices and small organizations are thus being replaced by groups and large-scale organizations, especially in larger urban areas. A medical group in its basic form is a partnership of physicians sharing equipment and offices at a common location and able to provide "one-stop shopping" by including a wide range of specializations in its membership. Two types that embody much greater organizational change, however, are health maintenance organizations (HMOs), the modern name for prepaid group practices, and preferred provider organizations (PPOs).

HMOs differ significantly from traditional physician groups: They include both hospitalization and outpatient services; their doctors and hospitals are a closed set of providers, meaning that the subscriber must seek services from within the HMO group; and their income derives from a fixed monthly or yearly amount per person enrolled, called a "capitation fee," thus combining the insurance and the services functions in the same organization. In exchange for a regular, fixed income, an HMO contracts to provide all of a wide range of normal medical and hospital services that may be needed

HMOs, PPOs, EPOs, and Hybrids

The original version (known as the staff model) of an HMO is a nonprofit organization that owns its own facilities, including both hospitals and physician office suites, and directly employs physicians on a salary basis. Very close is the group model, in which the organization also has its own facilities but contracts with a parallel group of physicians who retain greater professional autonomy by being salaried by their own organization rather than by the HMO. This kind of group contract arrangement is utilized in the best-known and the largest of all HMOs, Kaiser Permanente, which has over 6.5 million members, including nearly 5 million enrollees in California alone. A rather different group HMO is one that contracts with several traditional fee-for-service (FFS) group practices to provide medical services for its enrollees; those physicians are sometimes paid on an FFS basis, sometimes by capitation. Unlike the Kaiser type of group, their HMO work does not constitute their entire practice.

Yet another frequent type is the independent practice association (IPA). Originally a defensive ploy by local physician societies to compete with early HMOs, the IPA form became the choice of entrepreneurs establishing for-profit HMOs in the 1980s when private employers and the Reagan administration both encouraged HMOs. In 1990, the for-profits enrolled 47 percent of HMO members. The administration envisaged competition among HMOs as a primary means of holding down health care costs generally, and Medicare costs in particular, at a time when employers were becoming alarmed at the cost of employee health benefits. IPAs were the quick way to respond. They are much looser organizations than staff model HMOs and require less capital because they contract with hospitals (often paying negotiated per diem rates) rather than owning them and do not have to set up their own

by any of its enrollees. PPOs are made up of doctors and hospitals that agree to take a lowered fee in exchange for having a steady stream of patients referred by the insurer. And the patients are encouraged to use the listed providers because they receive a higher percentage of reimbursement than if they go to an outside source of care. For example, if reimbursement is usually 80 percent, the patient treated by a PPO doctor may have 90 percent covered. (For more on the proliferating variety of forms developing in the highly volatile HMO-PPO world, see the box.)

HMOs and PPOs exemplify the trend toward alternative delivery doctor offices. By 1990, IPAs were over 60 percent of all HMOs, though they attracted just one-third of enrollees.

The staff or group model HMO is both a provider and a group insurer in one organization; the IPA is really an insurance group that arranges for services with a limited set of providers.

About 550 HMOs now enroll over 36 million persons, over 1 million of whom are Medicare patients. However, the very rapid HMO growth of the late 1980s has been followed by a distinct slowdown in the early 1990s among both workers and Medicare enrollees. In 1990, HMO enrollments only grew 3 percent, and only 31 percent of the HMOs were open to Medicare patients. Although the share of HMO enrollees 10 years from now is not really predictable, HMOs are clearly here to stay—in one form or another. One of the emerging forms is a combination of HMOs and PPOs (called an open-ended HMO), in which there is no charge for using the HMO provider but partial reimbursement is given for using someone on an HMO-approved list of outside providers. Open-ended HMOs are sometimes called point-of-service arrangements.

PPOs are also spawning mutants, such as exclusive provider organizations (EPOs). Members of EPOs who use providers not on the approved list are not reimbursed. Sometimes an employer, instead of contracting with an outside PPO or HMO, sets up its own contractual network that may, however, be administered by an insurance company that has what is known as an ASO (administrative services only) contract with the employer.

And just to illustrate how much the organizational world of health care is in a state of flux, some employers have started to come full circle by getting their HMOs to agree to accept fee-for-service deals on their younger, healthier employees who don't often require the amount of care assumed under capitated fees to be the norm.

systems apparent in the early 1990s. They are also part of what Lawrence D. Brown calls the "managerial imperative," or the imposition of "administrative discretion between what patients demand and what physicians supply."[1] This extends far beyond organizational forms to include a great variety of intrusions by third-party payers into the traditionally sacrosanct doctor-patient relationship. In this broader sense, the term "managed care" is routinely used today to indicate one of the major contemporary aspects of health care that doctors find most frustrating: An insurance company's staff or a government contractor may look over the doctor's (or the hospital's) shoulder and haggle over whether a particular procedure is necessary (the required second-opinion provision) or how many hospital days should be allowed for a particular patient (called preadmission certification), based on a standardized response to a given diagnosis. We will examine this further in Chapter 6. Here we need only assert that the dominant force in the current health care policy scene is the effort by payers to limit their own costs.

Fitting into a Niche

A person feeling ill but lacking private-sector health insurance or adequate personal cash to pay for care thinks that being in the category of "sick person" should make one automatically eligible for public-sector medical financing. But life is not that simple: We have a bewildering array of program categories and criteria, resulting in multiple cracks through which one may fall. Having been in military service makes one eligible for one special set of health programs, a set that even includes a large number of hospital facilities designated specifically for veterans. Another criterion is tied to ethnicity: Being a native American makes one eligible for Indian Health Service care.

Medicare and Medicaid, intended for much larger segments of the population, receive most of the public attention. Medicare, which is called a "universal" program because eligibility is not income-related, is not as simple as we tend to assume. Although initiated as health insurance for those 65 or older, it now includes two other types of beneficiary whose eligibility is not age-determined: some of the permanently disabled, and persons with one (and only one) particular medical problem, end-stage renal disease requiring kidney dialysis. Even with these complications, it is a model of simplicity when compared with its sister program, Medicaid.

Although Medicaid is supposed to be the poor patient's health insurance plan, it serves only a minority of the poor (defined as living in a family whose income falls below the federally defined poverty level, e.g., $10,419 for a family of three and $13,359 for a family of four, in 1991). This is so for two reasons. First, Medicaid is a "categorical" program—meaning that in addition to being poor, one has to fit into one of several demographic or bureaucratic niches; that is, one must be on welfare or receive Supplemental Security Income (SSI) benefits or must be an elderly person reduced to poverty by nursing-home costs. Second, Medicaid is a cooperative national-state program and suffers from what might be termed excessive federalism.

Federalism as a Factor

The extraordinary complexity of Medicaid eligibility reflects the fact that it was established to fit the federalism component of our political system. Medicare is a national government program, and the scope of its services and its definitions of clientele cannot be varied by the states (although its payment relationship with physicians can be affected by the states through medical licensing requirements, and that relationship may affect the willingness of physicians to treat Medicare patients). Medicaid, however, is state operated but jointly financed by the national and state governments, with the national government's share (varying inversely with each state's income level) running from 50 to 68 percent and overall amounting to about 57 percent. This greater proportional contribution by the federal government to low-income states only partially compensates for the disadvantage these states face in trying to meet the needs of their Medicaid recipients. To receive the federal funds, each state must provide a minimum package of services, including inpatient and outpatient hospital services, rural health clinics, laboratory and x-ray services, skilled nursing, childhood screening, family planning, and physician services. All else (e.g., dental work, optometry, physical therapy, and preventive services) is at each state's option.

Most significant, most clients become eligible by first establishing welfare income eligibility, and that determination is entirely within the discretion of the states. So the *states* decide who among us will be eligible for help from this program established by the *nation*. The poorer a state, the less it can afford to contribute, and, generally, the lower the income at which one gets cut off from Medicaid. As of 1987, for example, family income had to be less than 38 percent of the poverty level in West Virginia, 55 percent in Maryland, but 82 percent in New York. In Alabama, a family of four was ineligible if its income was over $1,860 per year.

The combined state-federal mix thus produces unevenness and a tendency in recent years for the states to reduce the proportions of the needy who can qualify for Medicaid.

American Medicine Is Aggressive in Pursuing Cures

If we look at the explicitly medical characteristics of U.S. health care, the dominant practices can be summarized as an emphasis on acute episodes of reparable health problems over continuous care of chronic conditions—curing over preventing—and until quite recently, hospitalization over ambulatory care. These practices resulted partly from modern health insurance having been developed under hospital auspices, partly from insurance company coverage decisions, and partly from the demographic fact that we were a younger population when most features of the system were set in place. As medicine succeeds and we live longer, we also develop more of the chronic diseases—yet even Medicare as our primary program for the aged lacks provision for financing nursing-home and other long-term care needs, and very few medical schools require student exposure to geriatrics. Whether one's needs are acute or chronic, therefore, constitutes yet another set of categories having different access implications.

The least tangible characteristic of American health care, yet certainly among the most significant, is the attitudinal or cultural bias of the medical profession. It is the "Do something" ethic. Our medical practices and expectations are of a piece with the activist spirit that has characterized us as a people from the beginning.

Americans are not fatalists in general; in medicine, we assume that illness can be cured—and quickly. Morbidity resistant to cure bothers us; perhaps that partially explains our inadequate institutional response to chronic diseases. As a nation, we opened up a continent not by adapting to nature but by conquering it; in medicine, we are impatient with nature's own healing processes. We ask for antibiotics for head colds that are immune to them. We expect a pill for every ill.

Henry Ford, Alexander Graham Bell, Thomas Alva Edison—and in modern times the young turk founders of Apple Computers, Steven Jobs and Steven Wozniak—are among our leading folk heros. They all gave us practical technologies—and helped to create the myth of the technological fix. In medicine, this translates into such emphasis on diagnostic tests and machines that biomedical training today may be shortchanging the arts of taking a patient's history and diagnosing by means of the physician's clinical judgment based on personal examination of the patient.

In contemporary medicine, what names are recognized by the general public? Not those of leading diagnosticians and internists but the developers of wonder technologies and mind-boggling procedures—names like Michael DeBakey, Robert Jarvis, and William C. DeVries. These men are all associated in our minds with the ultimate in medical technology: the artificial heart, on which a quarter-billion dollars has been spent without much to show.

Comparison of actual physician fees with a scale based on costs, skills, and time involved has demonstrated that the technological-fix approach to medicine even ensures higher monetary rewards than less invasive approaches. This may be one reason why some surgeries—caesarian-section births and coronary bypasses being leading examples—are done at much greater frequency rates here than in other nations. And research has demonstrated that this resort to a technological fix when less aggressive approaches are available is sometimes not only unnecessary but potentially dangerous to the patient, simply because every operation creates an opportunity for infection.

"Aggressive"—that's the word that sums up American medical practice, both as doctors see their obligations under the Hippocratic oath and as patients see their own best chances for recovery, no matter what the illness. "For most physicians," writes Preston, "the dictum *primum non nocere* ('first, do no harm') is replaced by 'first, do something.'"[2]

Although this activist ethic is deeply embedded in our approach to health care, it has recently come under increasing challenge, most notably with regard to the use of expensive—and painful—operations and treatments to extend the lives of the terminally ill by only a few days or months and at a quality-of-life level that many patients themselves, particularly among the elderly, find not worthwhile. Deference to authority has never been a signal American trait, though it is greater when we face the mystique of the white-coated father-figure, and an insistence on making one's own medical choices is now sometimes surprisingly qualifying the traditional "Do something."

Reversing Incentives: Don't Do More, Do Less

Financial incentives are a crucial part of any health care system, perhaps especially when that system is predominantly market-oriented. So let's pull out for special attention here the conventional incentives of hospital and doctor financial relationships with patients and payers, and the changes now sharply modifying—even reversing—these relationships.

In the movement toward change, Medicare is the pacesetter. Its adoption in 1983 of a radically different way of paying for hospitalization inaugurated a major strategy for dampening the hospital cost escalation trend.

The diagnostic related group (DRG) system applies a fixed payment to the inpatient's diagnosed condition that corresponds to one of about 480 treatments and procedures. For example, DRG 79 is for respiratory infections, 103 is for a heart transplant, 134 is for hypertension, and 410 covers chemotherapy. The radical difference is that the payment is fixed by the diagnostic category rather than by how much time the patient spends in the hospital or which specific services and supplies are involved in the individual case. In other words, Medicare no longer pays on the *retrospective* basis of the detailed bill submitted by the hospital. Instead, it pays a *prospectively* set fee—one known in advance of the treatment—based on an analysis of typical hospitalization costs (especially average length of stay) involved in a particular diagnosis. (DRGs do not include the physician's charges.) In health care jargon, DRGs are one form of a prospective payment system (PPS).

If we now put together HMOs, mostly in the private sector, with DRGs (originated in the public sector but also being used in some private insurance plans), we can see that radical changes in physician and hospital incentives are developing in some parts of our system.

The Traditional System Encourages Maximum Utilization

In the traditional retroactive payment system, providers received payment on the basis of the particular services rendered, billed after the fact. Charges were accepted by third-party payers if they fit a pattern of being "customary, prevailing, reasonable" (in Medicare usage; or "usual, customary, and reasonable" in private insurance terminology)—which boils down to saying that whatever has usually been charged in a given area becomes the norm. And as fees are raised, the norm also rises.

Doctors and hospitals have thus had a powerful financial incentive to do *more*. The more separate services one provides, the more items one can bill for. Extra tests done in the doctor's own lab, or on which he takes a markup if done outside, mean extra income. Extra hospital days keep a hospital's beds occupied, and financial success for a hospital has traditionally rested on the occupancy rate, much as if it were a Holiday Inn. The patient may actually suffer from an unnecessary operation or from exposure to other patients' germs in a hospital but is not likely to suffer from lack of treatment—assuming he or she has insurance coverage or enough income to pay the bills.

But change the hospital's situation to prospective payment via DRGs and the incentive is reversed 180 degrees. Now the hospital does not benefit financially if it keeps the patient longer or supplies more tests or other services. Because the DRG category determines a flat fee, and that fee is known when the diagnosis is made, the hospital's interest lies in *minimizing* the number of services provided and the length of stay. If the hospital spends less on the patient than the DRG payment provides, it makes money; it if spends more, it loses money. In short, the less done, the larger the financial gain.

Patients thus get discharged from hospitals "quicker and sicker." A major study showed that the quality of care for Medicare patients—measured by treatments, diagnoses, and examinations—improved during the first few years of the DRG system. But the study also showed that the rate of those discharged in unstable condition had increased substantially and that those patients were 50 percent more likely to die within 90 days of discharge than were those stable at discharge. A mixed picture, and it only covers the first three years of DRGs, through 1986.

HMOs Also Reverse the Incentives

HMOs present the same incentive pattern for both their physician and hospital components as DRGs do for the treatment of Medicare hospital patients. An HMO's capitation income provides a fixed budget out of which all services are to be funded. If service costs are greater than payments, the HMO loses money; if payments are larger, the HMO makes money. Many of the newer HMOs are investor-owned, profit-seeking entities, so a good "bottom line" out of which to pay stockholder dividends is a major consideration. Even the not-for-profit HMO wants a surplus with which to purchase new equipment, modernize facilities, and pay salaries high enough to attract the physicians it wants on its staff.

Physician's incentives in an HMO setting are a more complex mixture. Some HMO physicians are on salary and thus presumably are freed from strong individual financial incentive in either direction. Cost-containment pressures are so great today, however, that physicians find themselves with other job-security incentives to do less: "production quotas" for the number of patients to be seen in a day and reviews by management if one is ordering more tests or doing more of a certain procedure than one's peers. However, such reviews are sometimes an important plus in preventing overutilization of resources in ways that do not help—and may even harm—the patients. The negative incentive for treatment in HMOs has another positive feature. It encourages the offering of preventive care—annual checkups, wellness programs, well-baby clinics, and strong child immunization programs for example—all of which may obviate much of the potential need for much more expensive curative treatment.

Medicare's Adoption of a Physicians' Fee Schedule

The newest change in financial incentives affects physicians operating outside of HMOs, whether as solo practitioners or in professional groups, when treating Medicare patients. This change does not reverse incentives, but it does reduce some fees and make all fees more predictable and uniform. This double-barreled innovation combines a relative value scale (RVS) and a volume performance standard (VPS). The RVS (being phased in from 1992 to 1996) will standardize payments and base them on resource costs (practice costs, specialized training, and work input, including time, skill, and judgment required), replacing the more arbitrary and uneven pattern of charges in the past. The need for rationalizing fees is clear if one looks at data on geographic variations that go far beyond local cost differences. For example, the prevailing charge in 1987 for an internist's comprehensive visit with a new patient ranged from $30 in Odessa, Texas, to $130 in San Diego, California; total hip replacement ranged from $1,663 in Milwaukee to $4,436 in Manhattan. Supposed to neither increase nor decrease Medicare physician costs overall, the RVS will decrease average payments for operations and high-tech procedures while raising the average for primary care visits, thus discouraging one kind of medicine in favor of another, with the advantage going to a less intrusive (and generally less expensive) mode of practice. General practitioners and family practice physicians are estimated to be major gainers; internists will come out even, and thoracic surgeons and gastroenterologists will be major losers. The VPS will set a soft cap on Medicare's total physician expenditure each year to discourage practitioners from the temptation to meet personal income targets by offering more services as a way of compensating for a lower fee per service. (Health care professionals, like the rest of us, need to make a living.)

What does it all add up to? The bulk of our privately insured health care still provides for payment modes that motivate the provider to maximize services. But with government programs taking the lead, a 180-degree turn is under way to design prospective payment systems that will give providers an incentive to minimize the services they provide. There can be a danger to the patient in either mode: Undertreatment is the concern under DRGs, per diems, and volume performance standards, but overtreatment under the motto of "Do everything possible—the insurance will pay for it" has been the equivalent danger of the traditional system. In either payment system, professional integrity backed up by societal monitoring is essential to protect the patient's health at the same time that we try to save the payer dollars.

How the System Developed: A Hospital-Oriented Sketch

The history of American health care—organizationally, as medical practice, and in its financing dimension—is in large part the history of the American hospital.

Our mental image of a modern hospital is that of a high-tech palace, the highest tech among them being university health sciences centers. But until the 1870–1910 period of transition, hospitals were closer to almshouses for the poor than facilities for medical cures. Because so many of the poor were sick (the causation worked both ways, then as now), public hospitals evolved out of almshouse infirmaries. Through the first half of the nineteenth century, the almshouses were places where the poor were more often sent to die than to be cured.

Then, with anesthesia after the 1840s, acceptance in the 1870s and 1880s of germ theory and of Joseph Lister's demonstration of the effectiveness of antiseptic procedures, and the development of x-rays for diagnoses in 1895, surgery became much safer and the number and range of operations mushroomed. These developments encouraged a new kind of hospital, one that middle-class and well-off patients of private physicians would use, because by about 1900 the hospital had developed an aseptic advantage over the home as a place to operate. Earlier, it had been safer to be treated at home, because the danger of infection was greater in nonaseptic hospitals with high proportions of patients with communicable diseases.

Adding to the developing emphasis on hospital care was a physician-training pattern that had, by the 1920s, come to require internships and encourage residencies (specialized training after receipt of the M.D. degree)—both pursued in acute care hospitals where a great range of patients, diseases, and surgical problems could be studied and treated. (The interns and residents worked on the poor, in wards; private doctors saw affluent patients in private rooms and middle-class paying patients in semiprivate rooms.) Having trained in hospitals, fledgling doctors saw it as simply natural that these facilities should be their "workshops."

The modern community hospital as we know it had now developed—along with the biomedical and technological bases of acute disease treatment—to a point that one had a better than even chance of benefiting from medical care. But along with effective care came much higher costs, costs too high to be met by philanthropic gifts to hospitals and too high for even many middle-class patients to meet comfortably out-of-pocket. Even before the Great Depression of the 1930s intensified and extended the financial problem, hospitals (expanding in number and thus often competing for patients in urban areas) were finding that the middle-class patients they needed to fill their beds were caught between their ineligibility for community-subsidized charity care and their inability to pay for all the technologically more sophisticated and medically more intensive care that the small numbers of the very affluent could command. It had become a real deprivation to go without medical care now that procedures had become sufficiently effective. But few could afford it as an unbudgeted, sudden, and unpredictable expenditure.

Dr. Kimball and the Prepaid Hospital Plan

The name Dr. Justin Ford Kimball might not head a general history's chapter on the important people of the 1920s, but he deserves a prominent place in the health care archives of this century. In 1929, Kimball—administrator of the Baylor University Hospital in Dallas, Texas—was worrying about unpaid patient bills and came up with an effective way for a group of Dallas schoolteachers (Kimball had earlier been the school superintendent) to *prepay* up to 21 days a year of hospital care by advance premiums of 50 cents a month.

As the Crash of 1929 became the Great Depression of the 1930s, hospital interest in Kimball's concept grew rapidly. By 1935—a time when voluntary hospitals still got almost three-fourths of their income directly from patients' out-of-pocket payments—there were already 15 hospital insurance plans in 11 states; by 1940, 4.4 million persons were enrolled in such plans, which had by then developed as the Blue Cross system under American Hospital Association (AHA) auspices. Although Blue Cross in time became independent of AHA and its units now bargain vigorously with hospitals over prices, the entire U.S. health care system received a lasting imprint from the hospital origins of prepaid care. Psychiatric coverage and nursing-home provision, for example, have been downplayed or absent in private health insurance over the years because the hospital-sponsored programs feared that inclusion of these categories of care would lead state governments (which were already attempting to meet needs in these specific areas) to fob them off onto the private sector. Given these origins, plus the fact that hospital bills were almost always far harder to face than the doctor's, it was not unnatural that such group health plans stressed hospitalization coverage. As an unanticipated consequence, doctors connived for many years with their patients to place them into hospitals to make them eligible for third-party payment for tests and x-rays that would not be covered on an outpatient basis. Further, because doctors and hospitals needed to achieve mutual cooperation for both medical and economic reasons, the physicians were able to shape Blue Cross so that their fees generally remained separate. Thus they used the hospital "workshop" but were not hospital employees. And this separation also established the pattern of private fee-for-service physicians following their patients into the hospital, as compared with the European system of developing in each hospital a corps of salaried specialists who performed hospital services on referral from the private-practice physicians (and without any financial incentive to maximize treatment).

The hospital's central role in the medical system was also enhanced by an early federal initiative to finance construction of community hospitals. The Hill-Burton Act (formally the 1946 Hospital Survey and Construction Act) was a more technologically oriented approach to health care needs than the proposals for publicly financed health insurance that had been advanced since the 1930s. The act provided for distribution of funds on a population and per capita income basis in each state; nearly $4 billion had been paid out by 1971.

A provision in the law intended to set limits became a justification for expansion. A limit was set of not more than 4.5 beds per thousand population, but the limit turned into a target (because no state had yet even come close to that high a ratio) that provided an official standard the hospital industry could use to further its growth aims. Ambulatory care had no such legislative standard to act as a rallying point for federal aid.[3]

In time, insurance coverage of doctors' fees developed under the Blue Shield banner. With Blue Cross hospital-stimulated and Blue Shield physician-stimulated (and consumers not in any explicit way represented in either organization), American health insurance developed as a system emphasizing "doing well by doing good." Patients got insurance they very much needed as more sophisticated medicine came to mean more expensive medicine, threatening family budgets. Providers got greater assurance of payment plus a position of leverage from which they could dominate the shaping of a private health care system.

By World War II, private insurers had joined Blue Cross in offering a variety of plans, and the United States was well along its unique path of private, employment-based group health insurance. The consolidating element of this direction came as an adjunct to wage controls in World War II, when it was decreed that fringe benefits such as pensions and health insurance would be exempt from wage ceilings. Health care became a major bargaining element at a time when companies were prospering on war orders and had subsidized health care benefits in the form of a tax-deductible business expense. Uncle Sam gave a double stimulus to private insurance, thus helping to focus the entire system on a middle-class employment base. As a result of both patient need and entrepreneurship by providers and insurers, shortly after the end of the war there were 19 million Blue Cross enrollees, and by 1950, 77 million people had some kind of hospitalization insurance and 54 million had coverage for surgery.

The combination of insurance coverage and changes in medical practice stressing use of hospitals as the only proper and safe place to operate created a dramatic shift in where procedural medicine was practiced. In 1935, half of all births were still accomplished in the home, but as early as the 1950s, 96 percent of newborns were being delivered in hospitals.

The 1950s also, paradoxically, saw the beginnings of the seismic shift to outpatient care, including free-standing "surgicenters," of which there were about 1,200 in 1991. The hospital share of health insurance premium money went down from 70 percent in 1950 to barely half by 1983, and hospital admissions between 1980 and 1990 fell by 26 percent for those under 65 and, in 1983–1987, by 16 percent for the elderly.

Although some new technologies use less invasive procedures and thus permit outpatient or office-based treatment without danger of infection, others (transplant procedures, for example) will require extended hospitalization. Bruce C. Vladeck, president of the United Hospital Fund of New York, makes a strong case for a revitalized future role for hospitals as community coordinators of health care. Such coordination would involve looking at the patient's needs regardless of where those needs would be met. Hospitals would serve as institutional backups for nonhospital providers—not only when things went wrong in a surgicenter but also as more services, such as intravenous medications, became available through home health services. Already, acute care hospitals are refilling emptied beds by turning wards into nursing-home units, and many are themselves running home health services. Hospitals may indeed become more vital than ever as the unifying element for all the disparate strands in the fragmented world of specialization and niche-filling entrepreneurial organizations.

National Health Insurance as an Emerging Issue

Private third-party coverage—overwhelmingly provided as a largely employer-financed employee benefit—was now clearly *the* "American way," having developed in a clear field from 1929 until 1965, when the publicly sponsored models of Medicare and Medicaid entered the picture. Private insurance companies worried about a perceived incentive for patients to overuse the system because the employer was paying for the care; but until the 1970s the national emphasis remained on extending coverage, not on worrying about possibly avoidable costs.

Attempts to establish a universal, publicly financed health care system had been made sporadically since before World War I but were turned back each time. In the 1930s, the social policy priority of the depression years went to pensions. President Franklin D. Roosevelt decided that he could not politically afford to add medical care to the Social Security package in 1935. When it was realized after World War II that many millions of persons were untouched by the growth of employment-related health insurance, another major effort to achieve national health insuance (NHI) was mounted by President Harry S. Truman. But he was defeated in 1949 by an AMA-sponsored public relations campaign.

Advocates of NHI then fell back and regrouped, finally opting to push for legislation geared to the needs of specific groups that had obvious needs and for whom there was some public sympathy: the elderly and single mothers with small children. The landslide victory of President Lyndon B. Johnson in 1964 carried a large Democratic majority into Congress, and Medicare and Medicaid became law in 1965. Even then the pattern of private professional dominance was so strong that the legislation forswore any governmental intervention in the existing mode of practicing medicine—which was taken to include modes of hospital payment. Medicare further reinforced the hospitals' role in the system by including in its payment rates reimbursement for depreciation of capital—despite the beginnings of awareness that it was time to use whatever leverage government had to move the system toward ambulatory care.

The inauguration of Medicare and Medicaid muffled the demand for universal health insurance for some years. Further, the call for improved access was drowned out by what began as a limited budgetary concern of Medicare, a concern soon echoed by corporations rebelling against employee health benefit costs. By the late 1970s we had what we now know as the cost-containment crisis.

Cost Control as a First Priority

The miracles of medicine are real enough, but they rarely come cheap—and less so all the time, it seems. A cochlear implant for the severely deaf costs $14,000 for the electronic gear and another $10,000–$15,000 for the implantation surgery and hospitalization. In 1988 dollars, liver transplants cost $175,000, heart transplants $83,000, and saving a premature baby with severe problems might run $250,000. And when cost-increasing incentives dominate the way we pay for care, it's small wonder that cost containment has become "Job 1" in health policy.

Cost Versus Access

Just as cost problems were achieving number one priority status among both private and governmental payers, the advocates of broader access for those we can call the medically disadvantaged were, paradoxically, able to stimulate new public concern for greater equity in health care distribution. So now the battle was on.

In the 1982 recession the media publicized loss of health insurance because of job layoffs and the deterioration of Medicaid as states kept reducing the income levels at which the needy became ineligible. Congress responded by mandating in 1985 (in what is informally known as the COBRA continuation program) that those losing health insurance by losing their jobs, or their dependent relationship to a jobholder with insurance, could at least continue their insurance at the group rate for a period of 18 months to 3 years, depending on the person's category, if they paid the premium themselves. Not much, but something on the positive side. Congress also acted to improve Medicaid access for pregnant women and children.

Public opinion polls in the 1980s indicated a strong public expectation that the pattern of expanding health insurance established since the 1930s would continue and certainly would not be reversed. And the explosion of high-tech inventions increased both public demand for the latest in medical miracles and public fear that families needing the wonder treatments would not be able to afford them.

By the beginning of the 1990s, therefore, there were strong contradictory currents: to extend public provision of medical care to obviously needy clients lacking their own resources—especially pregnant women and young children—and to rein in costs. The 1991 recession, with a loss of white-collar service jobs and an increasing awareness that most of the medically uninsured were working people, shifted the balance a bit more toward emphasis on the coverage problem once again, but continuing strong antitax sentiment and a weak private economy made it clear that cost would remain a decisive factor in determining what was done.

Cross Subsidies and the Loss of Community

Cross subsidies are the vanishing lubricant of the system. They constitute the final piece in the puzzle of a nation that thinks health care should be a personal right but that leaves a substantial portion of its population unprotected and faces a deteriorating situation despite the highest expenditures in the world. Cross subsidies have been the hidden linkage between cost and access in the post–World War II world, but the chain is being broken, contributing strongly to the current crisis.

Very simply, a cross subsidy occurs when a hospital that receives no payment from a patient, or less than its costs on a patient whose coverage is from Medicare or Medicaid, shifts the unpaid costs to patients whose insurance programs pay on the traditional basis of the "customary" charge. In essence, this is an updated version of the classic sliding-fee system used by individual doctors in preinsurance days who charged wealthy patients more than necessary in order to feel able to treat low-income patients who could not pay regular costs. It is the traditional way in which the medical care system fulfills its professional responsibility to be sensitive to community needs rather than just be part of a commodity market.

All insurance is, by nature, a way of sharing risks, and we do not object to paying a fire insurance premium on our home that goes to pay the claim of someone else unfortunate enough to have a fire if we are lucky enough to avoid the catastrophe ourselves. The same attitude was true in health care, with the added tolerance for up-per-to-lower income redistribution because of the recognition that illness is not confined to those who can afford treatment. The lessened sense of community that seems to afflict us as a side effect of glorifying individual accumulation of money in the 1980s, joined with very real financial problems for both providers and patients as we enter the 1990s with a slow economy, has sharply reduced the willingness of third-party payers to continue the cross subsidies that bridge the gap between health care needs and inability to pay the ever-escalating costs of treatment.

The uncompensated-care problem caused by this gap is rapidly worsening. The American Hospital Association estimates that the combination of Medicaid payment shortfalls and unsponsored-care costs jumped from $3.5 billion in 1980 to $13.2 billion in 1989.

This leads hospitals to try to shift such costs to those who can pay, but the increased need to shift costs is unfortunately accompanied by greater difficulty in doing so as hospitals have had to accept discounted payments from large private payers for competitive reasons. As these payers have developed stronger leverage over the providers, they have narrowed the use of their power so that it serves only their own institutional imperatives. Because hospitals are caught between private and public third-party payers—each insisting that it will cover costs only for its own group—hospitals, as well as physicians, are losing their ability to act as members of a health care community even when the desire to supply care to all continues.

What do all these characteristics and trends add up to? A health care system that abounds with technological marvels and has a very full complement of skilled professionals and well-equipped institutions to provide treatment. But this system lacks a private-public infrastructure of finance and organization adequate to include all Americans in its delivery pattern despite the highest per capita costs in the world.

Now it's time to look at the symptoms of trouble in detail.

Part Two

Understanding
the Problems

3
What Are the Problems?

I may be active and vigorous yet develop an abdominal pain indicating a health problem; or I may show no external symptoms yet be in the first stages of one of the chronic diseases, such as cancer, that has a long gestation period.

So it is with the American health care system. Healthy and diseased aspects coexist, and some of its underlying problems may not be symptomatically apparent. Before we can determine the causes of the tragic shortfall between our potential for superb health care and the faltering actuality, we need to examine the symptoms of systemic failure in both the access and cost dimensions.

Access: Who Has It? Who Does Not?

The most astounding fact about access in a wealthy nation like ours whose public asserts overwhelmingly that it believes access to health care is a "right" is the size of the uninsured population (nearly 36 million persons). Today one's access to health care very largely mirrors one's access to health insurance.

Who are all these uninsured people—the unemployed? No.

Although nearly 90 percent of all Americans have insurance through employment, being employed is no guarantee of having health coverage. As noted earlier, more than three-fourths of the uninsured are workers or their dependents. Another 2 million uninsured are uninsurable because of excluded or preexisting conditions. This partly explains another surprising finding: Nearly one-fourth of the uninsured are in families with incomes of $30,000 or more.

These 1989 data reveal that approximately 7 million more persons are uninsured for health care than in 1980. After a steady increase in health insurance coverage from the 1930s onward, we have recently moved backward. The 1990–1991 recession (like that of 1982) has further affected the numbers; more than 17 percent of the total population may now be without insurance.

But, one might ask, aren't we at least seeing that our children are covered? It appears that we have been falling behind even there. A recent government study found that between 1977 and 1987 the proportion of uninsured children (under age 18) rose from 13 to 18 percent (8 million to 11 million persons under 18). In poor and low-income families the gap increased from 21 to 31 percent uninsured. The proportion of uninsured is probably higher now.

Yet another disturbing dimension of the medically uninsured population is its ethnic skewing: A 1991 report estimated that 10.2 percent of non-Hispanics were uninsured; the figure for Puerto Ricans was 15.5 and for Mexican-Americans 36.9 percent. Blacks had the highest percentage at 19.7.

What does being uninsured mean in people's lives? It can mean being "dumped" from a hospital emergency room: The hospital does a "wallet biopsy," learns that the patient has no coverage, and transfers the person to the nearest public facility. Although both federal law and statutes of a number of states forbid transfer for financial reasons of a person in unstable medical condition, anecdotal evidence of dumping continues to accumulate, and enforcement of the laws is apparently less than vigorous.

Findings from a 1988 survey of 60 public hospitals and from 1990 studies of two California public hospital emergency rooms show these symptoms of institutional illness:

- Over half of all out-patient visits were by uninsured patients, often using the hospital as a family doctor equivalent;
- ER patients in the 1988 survey waited an average of five hours for transfer to a hospital ward bed and in some cases waited 3 to 10 days. The average wait to be seen by a doctor was 3.5–6.4 hours in the two 1990 studies but was sometimes as long as 17 hours. (Yet Americans express shock when told that Canadians and the British have to be on waiting lists for *nonemergency* elective surgeries!)

If one has a serious medical condition and is successfully admitted to a hospital, does the difference between the insured and the uninsured then become insignificant? Unfortunately, no. A major 1991 study of almost 600,000 cases found that insurance status was closely linked to use of certain high-cost and/or high-discretion procedures (e.g., coronary artery bypass surgery, knee replacement, hip replacement). The uninsured were 29 to 75 percent less likely to be treated with one or another of these procedures than equivalent patients privately insured. Further, in 13 of 16 specific groups examined, the uninsured had from 44 to 124 percent higher risk of in-hospital mortality.

The one consoling element in this report is that in nondiscretionary essential services the discrepancy disappeared, suggesting that physicians do not apply an economic screen when the indications of medical need are unambiguously clear. However, that may not always be the case, for another recent study of hospital-discharge data revealed that among persons hospitalized for heart attacks, the uninsured were 57 percent more likely to die than those with fee-for-service insurance and 48 percent more likely to die than those with HMO coverage. They were also less likely to get such treatments as angioplasty or bypass surgery.

Do we do better by sick newborn babies? Maybe not. A recent study found that uninsured sick newborns had 28 percent fewer resources devoted to their needs and were discharged more than two days sooner than insured babies even though they probably needed longer stays.

One more example of the consequences of being uninsured: Forty percent of uninsured persons admitted to hospitals in the District of Columbia in a recent period could have avoided hospital care if they had received primary care at an earlier point. Of insured patients, this was true for only 12 percent. Even if we allow for personal responsibility in some proportion of these cases, the correlation between insurance and treatment is strong enough to show that lack of insurance creates access barriers even to ordinary care, not just to treatment with expensive life-saving surgical procedures. Given urban sprawl and inadequate public transportation, it is often difficult for the uninsured, for example, working single mothers, to reach the public hospital that is often the only place they can get even primary treatment.

These are some of the problems faced by the medically uninsured, most of whom are poor even if working. If one is poor and not working, does Medicaid constitute adequate insurance? Hardly. Let's look more closely at this supposed "safety net."

Medicaid: Poor Insurance for Poor People

The first big hole in the net is Medicaid's failure to cover a majority of the poor. Unfortunately, the program's first years seem to have been its best in this respect. The percentage of the Medicaid-insured poor shows a downward progression:

Year	Percent Covered
1965	76
1975	63
1991	38 (est.)

Medicaid eligibility begins with welfare eligibility—that is, being on the rolls of the Aid to Families with Dependent Children (AFDC) program. That has generally meant being a low-income single parent (more than 20 states did not provide AFDC if the parents were together but both unemployed) with children under 18. And it almost always means having an income far below even the official poverty levels, for each state sets its own AFDC eligibility criteria. Forty-nine percent of poverty is the average eligibility requirement, but there is great variation, as noted in Chapter 2. From the variation in the degree of poverty that triggers eligibility emerges a second category consisting of the "medically needy." These are defined as those who fit the AFDC categories but whose incomes are above the state AFDC cutoff point. Such persons may become eligible by "spending down"—using up enough of their own resources on medical care to be reduced to the prescribed degree of poverty.

In some states there is also a category known as Medically Indigent Adults (MIAs), who are persons 18–64, single or married, but without dependent children. As it operates in California, for example, the program for MIAs primarily assists the working poor by applying a sliding-scale fee schedule to persons not fitting any other category. They may be employed in low-wage jobs by employers not offering health insurance or whose insurance is too limited in coverage. Most of them are among the very poor, like regular Medicaid recipients, but not fitting the regular categories of welfare.

The federal government also requires that the states give Medicaid eligibility to the low-income blind, elderly, and disabled who are receiving income assistance from SSI (Supplementary Security Income), which has a nationally set threshold at 75 percent of poverty, thus creating an "upper tier" category in most states.

Sometimes one has to establish dual eligibility in both Medicare and Medicaid to meet very clear needs. The over-65 person requiring basic nursing-home care, but not a doctor's daily attention, cannot obtain that care from Medicare. To obtain it from Medicaid, she or he must often use up a lifetime's savings to pay privately for nursing-home care and dispose of almost all assets in order to spend down sufficiently to be eligible. In one study, almost 30 percent of Medicaid nursing-home residents had begun as private-pay patients but had exhausted their own resources, often within a few months.

Even after all these options are applied, a *majority* of the poor are left hanging in midair without the famed "safety net" of Ronald Reagan's rhetoric.[1]

Beyond categories of persons eligible for Medicaid, there are categories of treatments covered or not by Medicaid. Although the federal government requires that each state-run Medicaid program include certain basic hospital and physician services, there is great variation in the range of specialized services offered. For example, as of 1990 optometry services were covered in all states except Mississippi and Tennessee. Hospital emergency services were covered in most states, but not in Connecticut, Georgia, North Carolina, or Pennsylvania, among others—but all of these did offer clinic services.

These eligibility stipulations demonstrate that Medicaid suffers from extreme unevenness in its application. But that's not all. Even if one is part of the lucky minority eligible for Medicaid, the eligibility card is often only a patient's license to hunt for a physician or a hospital because many providers do not accept Medicaid patients or limit the Medicaid proportion of their practices. In California, 80 percent of private physicians were not taking prenatal patients covered by MediCal (as Medicaid is termed in that state) until the reimbursement rate was doubled and a recruitment program was established in 1990. Recent congressional mandating of coverage for small children is based on the assumption that the mother can find an accepting pediatrician. But a 1989 national survey by the American Academy of Pediatrics revealed a 1978–1989 decline from 85 percent to 77 percent of pediatricians accepting Medicaid patients. As we increase legal eligibility we seem to be decreasing physician willingness to treat.

Lack of Care from Coast to Coast

The human consequences of being uninsured and of ineffective Medicaid insurance for the poor are clear from coast to coast. Newspaper
accounts tell the tale.

• A Los Angeles walk-in hospital clinic began turning away patients
for the first time in its 58-year history in September of 1990 after the
newest in a series of budget cuts in its indigent health care program.
Screening criteria are being applied to accomplish a kind of triage
(medical prioritizing) to ensure that treatment will be given at least to
those whose symptoms are likely to escalate into a life-threatening
condition within 48 hours. At specialty clinics (for diabetes, heart
disease, asthma, etc.), the wait for appointments would be up to 12
weeks, said health officials.

• In New York City, three subsidized gynecological clinics operated
by a nonprofit volunteer agency with a mix of city, federal, and private
funds were closed in March 1991, leaving thousands of women who
were on Medicaid—or without insurance but able to pay a low clinic fee
(though not a private physician's charges)—without anyplace to go for
Pap smears, birth control pills, examinations, and pregnancy and AIDS
counseling.

Only 25 percent of New York State's physicians regularly treat Med-

Ironically (in a program originated for small children and their
mothers), Medicaid has (by default) become the nation's long-term
care program for the elderly, and this has been accomplished at the
expense of the children. Seventy-five percent of Medicaid funds pay
for nursing-home care for the poor elderly and disabled, who are
only 28 percent of all Medicaid recipients. In fiscal 1988, the average
program expenditure per child was $584, but $9,800 per elderly
person.

Medicare, Too, Has Problems

Medicare has clearly been a very successful program. Its primary
eligibility requirement—having attained the age of 65—is simple,
requires no means test or administrative hoops, and is basically
uniform throughout all the states. Medicare offers substantial hospitalization and physician services benefits and has made a tremendous difference in the lives of its beneficiaries, both medically and in
reducing debilitating fears of fiscal catastrophe because of illness.

However, Medicare's cost-sharing provisions and a few major gaps
in its coverage mean that access to care is far from universal both in
terms of care beneficiaries receive and in terms of eligibility. The

icaid patients—in good part because although the state spends $12 billion annually on Medicaid (almost twice California's expenditure for a larger population), its fees to doctors ($11 for many visits) are extremely low. However, its fees to nursing homes ($112 a day) are second only to New Hampshire's—a measure of the political strength of the nursing-home industry. Put these elements together and the sickness of New York's system can be expressed as an extreme case of the national intergenerational pattern mentioned previously: In New York, children are 46 percent of the eligible population and use 13 percent of the Medicaid dollars; the elderly are 13 percent of the eligibles and use 41 percent of the dollars, mostly for nursing homes.

• A Chicago physician, Dr. Quentin Young, says that he restricts the number of Medicaid patients he sees because he would otherwise go broke. He calls his policy a mix of "reality and shame" and comments that Medicaid patients "are shunted about. Either they are rejected by competent physicians or are very often put into clinics that abuse the system, with very little gain in health."

It is fair to say that the health care system is in a state of trauma for both the Medicaid-insured and the uninsured. Is the situation much better for the elderly because of Medicare? Yes—but Medicare, too, is not without real problems.

first-day deductible for hospitalization, $204 in 1981, had risen to $652 by 1992. The physician services (Part B of Medicare) monthly premium rose to $31.80 and is scheduled to reach $46.10 in 1995. There is also a $100 annual deductible (raised in 1990 from $75).

The major gaps are in long-term care (nursing homes), prescription medications, and coverage for hearing aids. Nursing-home care—which Medicare does not cover except in limited cases such as a short-term stay after prolonged hospital treatment—costs $25,000 a year, and even more in some cities. Hundreds of thousands of elderly persons would be faced with a catastrophic access problem if Medicaid had not been turned (rather inadvertently) into a long-term care (LTC) supplement to Medicare. Prescription drugs are another large drain on the elderly's resources, which Congress tried to make less onerous with its ill-fated 1988 catastrophic care law, repealed after a voter revolt over its mode of financing.

As a result of coverage exclusions and cost-sharing increases, the elderly now spend about $2,400 a year (18 percent of income) out-of-pocket on health care needs—which is about the same proportion as before Medicare was enacted. For the poor and near-poor, those direct costs are a not-inconsiderabie deterrent to obtaining care. This hardship is mitigated, it is true, by the Medigap private insurance policies (to pay deductibles and copayments), which two-thirds of the elderly purchase, and by 1990 legislation requiring that state Medicaid programs pick up the tab for Medicare premiums and deductibles for over-65 persons below the U.S. poverty line.

The uninsured, the poor on Medicaid, and the elderly on Medicare all belong to special categories, and they are all dependent on a mix of private charity and public programs. The health care system clearly leaves much to be desired in meeting their needs, and coverage variations are so great as to be a major scandal in the eyes of all who trouble to look at the irrational unevennesses.

But surely, one might think, things are better for the majority of Americans who are privately insured, mostly through employee benefit programs. Well, yes—but symptoms of declining health are also developing in this top tier of health insurance.

Employee Benefit Health Insurance: The Strongest Sector Is Getting Weaker

Most of us know from our own experience and that of family and friends that for those under 65 the predominant way to pay for health care bills is by coverage supplied by an employer as an employment benefit. As noted in Chapter 2, the combination of increases in both cost and effectiveness of medical care from World War II onward, plus a strong push during the war for health insurance as an employee benefit, started a trend that continued unabated until the recessions of the early 1980s and 1991 reduced the percentage of those insured. In addition to the recessions and slow growth, there is also some loss of workplace-related insurance as the structure of the economy shifts from unionized manufacturing establishments to nonunion service industries, the lower-wage segments of which much less often include such benefits.

The big story in the early 1990s concerns shrinkage in the populations that employers include in their coverage and rising financial hurdles to care because of increased cost-sharing imposed on employees.

From 1982 to 1986, the picture was quite mixed. Coverage for vision, hearing, and alcohol abuse increased, but free choice of provider declined as HMO and PPO enrollments were pushed. The percentage of workers required to contribute to their health insurance premiums rose from 29 to 46 percent for individual coverage and from 51 to 65 percent for families.

Still, as of 1986 more than half of employees had first-dollar (i.e., total reimbursement with no deductible) hospital coverage and free insurance for themselves; a third had free family coverage too.

About that time, however, change for the worse quickened its pace. For the four years ending in 1988, a survey of over 200 large firms showed an increase from 51 to 70 percent in deductibles and a rise from 26 to 40 percent in plans calling for 20 percent copayments. There is evidence that cost-sharing at the point of treatment deters early use of health care, sometimes to the point that more serious (and more expensive) treatment becomes necessary.

Firms are increasingly offering only a choice of HMOs and PPOs. Southern California Edison, for example, imposes a 30 percent copayment if the patient goes outside the PPO "network," and Allied Signal arranges a network contract with Cigna insurance that calls for a deductible of 3 percent of salary. One survey showed a decrease in the proportion of free-choice plans from 85 percent in 1984 to 40 percent in 1988. Aetna Life and Casualty Company, in cooperation with its employer customers, reduced from 64 to 22 the percentage of those it covered in traditional plans just in the single year 1989. Even more financial hurdles in the way of access appear to be on the way. A 1990 survey by *Business and Health* magazine found that among its respondents, 70–80 percent planned to increase employee premiums, deductibles, or copayments during that year. Even greater access problems are hitting dependents and retirees as employers—quite understandably from a bottom-line business standpoint—seek to restrict their mushrooming health care costs by concentrating on currently active employees. Competition for good workers justifies benefits for active workers, but not those for retirees, runs one argument—to which labor's advocates respond that retiree benefits are just a form of deferred compensation, in the absence of which cash wages should be higher. The National Association of Manufacturers reported in 1989 that almost one-sixth of its survey respondents were then requiring the employee to pay the entire premium for dependent coverage—which means many dependents will go without insurance. Many companies are eliminating dependent coverage for new employees, and others may soon reduce dependent-plan scope by excluding mental health and substance abuse benefits.

Those who retire in the future before they reach Medicare eligibility will see their insurance coverage reduced the most. Early retirees compare poorly with active workers: Only 1 out of 50 small businesses gives retiree health benefits. By 1989, 40 percent of firms responding to the annual A. Foster Higgins survey of 2,000 employers were no longer offering health benefits for retirees under 65. Ten percent of the firms had decreased their benefits in the preceding two years. Fifteen percent had increased the employee premium share, and almost as many said they would do so in 1990.

One example of the extent of recent cost-shifting onto employees: General Motors (GM) retirees (although still more fortunate than most) were paying up to $750 out-of-pocket in 1991 versus $0 three years earlier. (GM, with an aging work force and ever-increasing competition, faces some real problems: Its health care plans cover more dependents and retirees than active employees, the ones whose productivity pays for everyone's insurance.) The courts generally deny a firm the right to cancel a medical benefit in existence when one was hired if the recruiting and benefits literature did not make clear from the beginning that such benefits were cancellable. So some companies are now announcing that newly hired employees should not expect health benefits when they retire. And it appears that a popular strategy for a growing number of companies (one-third of respondents in a 1990 *Business and Health* survey) will be to move from the unpredictable inflationary costs of existing health plans to what is known as a "defined contribution plan," or DCP. As is also becoming the style with corporate pension plans, the DCPs for health care guarantee a certain dollar contribution from the employer but not a certain level of benefits. For instance, an employer might promise to pay $200 per month toward a health insurance premium. When the cost rises above that, the employee is responsible for making up the difference or sees the benefits trimmed. A variant, also derived from pension analogies, is to relate retiree health benefits to length of service—perhaps treating 25 years as an expected work-life span—and on that basis pay a contribution of 4 percent of health plan costs for each year worked. According to this strategy, the 25-year employee would get full payment, but the 13-year worker would get only 52 percent of the premium paid by the employer.

Some active workers face even worse problems: revisions in the way insurance companies write health care policies and the increasing categories of persons being excluded from coverage.

Blue Cross–Blue Shield began as a nonprofit organization with a public service motif and stressed "community rating" in setting its premiums. This meant that all employee groups had the same rates regardless of the age or health experience of the particular firm's work force. Although some "Blues" still offer community rating, the majority have moved toward "experience rating" (i.e., differential rates geared to the health care experience of a particular work-force group) to meet competition that developed from profit-oriented commercial insurers. With increasing emphasis by employers on cost containment, all insurers are under great pressure to lower rates, partly by demanding discounts from providers but also by selecting out potentially riskier patients. Fragmenting group rates in this manner saves money for employers with young, healthy work forces and few retirees; but it also means much higher premiums and cost-sharing for employees in other corporate groups, with some simply becoming unable to afford the same level of care they once had.

The next steps along this path are toward experience rating at the individual level—even to the point of adjusting rates for possible *future* experience. It has long been usual that many employer-sponsored plans have varying premiums for single members, couples, and families with children, but the fragmentation is now being extended by insurers to the point of differentiating groups by their occupations, locations, and ages, especially for small businesses. Some insurers even exclude certain individuals from coverage within a group—such as an employee's small child with a heart murmur. Refusal to pay for a particular treatment even of a covered employee is also occurring as employers balk at paying for expensive treatments when the chances of success are low.

Occupational blacklisting is one of the latest ways that health insurers try to escape insuring possibly expensive employees. Among those blacklisted with one or another insurer are gas station attendants, restaurant employees, taxi drivers, arts and dance groups, and florists—and even doctors, dentists, and nurses, who are said to have a high rate of health care utilization because of their special knowledge. The exclusions have gone so far that even some insurance industry executives are expressing real concern about what is happening to accessibility—and to their reputations.

Another tack recently being taken by some insurers to reduce their risks is to use rapidly developing knowledge about genetics to exclude persons with "suspect genes." The extent of genetic discrimination is known mostly through anecdotal evidence so far, although a special study is now under way to measure its pervasiveness and find ways to stop it. Some discrimination is based on ignorance: A person known as a carrier of a defective gene is not affected by the disease and cannot produce a child with the disease unless the other parent is also a carrier.

The final element in this catalog of reduced health insurance availability is one that strikes even employees with high-end traditional indemnity insurance. It is the increasing practice of disallowing claims for reimbursement of prescription medicines when the particular application of the medicine has not received explicit approval from the U.S. Food and Drug Administration (FDA). For example, alpha interferon, approved for treatment of hairy cell leukemia, is also used for renal cell cancer.

Many of these applications are state-of-the-art and accepted among leading physicians. Pharmaceutical firms, however, do not bother to get approvals for each use that develops after a drug's first clearance because of the high cost in dollars and time to go through the process. Insurers and employers are now arbitrarily labeling all such uses "experimental." The result is sometimes a strong deterrent against treatment with an effective medication because of an unexpected cost.

Put all of this together and it is clear that lack of access to health insurance and therefore to free-from-worry health care now affects middle- and upper-income well-employed people, too, not just the poor or the unemployed. It is fast becoming a case not simply of whether one is insured but how well and of what unexpected or unpredictable exclusions one may face when medical problems strike. Some of the private insurer marketing ploys to avoid higher-risk subscribers are creating a backlash in informed quarters, and reform efforts are under way in some states to prevent some of the more outrageous exclusion patterns. As I write, however, insurers are succumbing to pressures of competition and not to conscience or a sense of community. The access gap may get worse before it gets better.

Health Care Leads the Inflation Index

To the patient and the physician, quality and accessibility of treatment take priority over cost in the triad of health care objectives. To those who pay the bills—mostly employers, state and national governments, and insurers, but increasingly some of the unluckier patients who are un- or underinsured—cost has become the overwhelming focal point for policy changes. Employers in a harshly competitive global business world and governments whose budgets are drowning in red ink see health care as an ogre looming over them. Consider some of the symptomatic figures:

- National health spending jumped from $540 billion in 1988 to $666 billion in 1990. For 1991, $738 billion was the early estimate; a further increase to $817 billion was projected for 1992. The latter figure might be 14 percent of GNP, because the rate of economic growth is expected to be so much lower than that of health care.
- The 1990 figure is an increase of 10.5 percent over that of the previous year, and the 1991 estimate is another 10 percent jump—despite strenuous efforts to reduce the rate of cost increase.
- In individual terms, 1991 health expenditures approached $3,000 per person—far more than twice what they had been in 1980 even after discounting for inflation.

Because everything else seems to go up in price every year, perhaps these figures are not as bad as they seem? Wrong. See the table of health care inflation factors in Chapter 2. Why health care costs rise faster than those of most other services and products is explored in the next chapter. Here we simply note as a symptom the fact of more rapid inflation. This results in another systemic problem: A larger share of total national resources has to be devoted to health care each year. Health care's share of GNP was 5.9 percent in 1965, the year that Medicare and Medicaid were legislated. By 1980, the figure had risen to 9.1, by 1985 to 10.5, and in 1990 it went over 12 percent. Particularly when economic growth is slow—or nonexistent—this means a real loss of the opportunity to do other things with our financial resources.

If we zero in on the components of who is paying for these increases, we can quickly see the sources of business and government anguish. Some facts on the government sector:

- Estimated federal expenditures on Medicare for 1990 were $110 billion, up 14 percent from 1989. If present trends are not changed, the Medicare Hospital Fund (Part A) may be bankrupt by 2005.

- Combined federal-state costs of Medicaid were $68 billion, the states' share being $30 billion. Thanks partly to congressionally mandated eligibility expansions, Medicaid is now the fastest-growing component in state budgets, climbing an astonishing 18 percent in 1990 and running at a 25 percent rate in the early months of 1991.

In the employer-sponsored sector, corporate health expenditures averaged $3,605 per employee in 1991, an increase of 12 percent in one year according to an A. Foster Higgins survey. Another survey, by Hewitt Associates, found that large insurers anticipated that FFS rates would go up 22 percent in 1992 and HMO rates almost 14 percent.

The loudest squawks are coming from the extremes of the business world: from giant automobile manufacturers and from small businesses.

- Employee benefit health costs ran $689 per vehicle at General Motors, $702 at Chrysler, and $537 at Ford according to a late 1990 report.

- A survey by the National Federation of Independent Businesses (NFIB) revealed that health insurance premiums for the small businesses represented by the federation increased from 20 to 200 percent in 1989. And insurance industry figures showed small-business premiums ranging from $1,000 to $10,000 per employee. One result of such increases was that the percentage of NFIB member firms offering health insurance stopped growing after 1986, after steady growth for some years before that.

It's not just the third-party payers for whom rising health care costs signal a system in distress. Hospitals, as the biggest single type of provider needing to have its bills paid (40 percent of health care expenses), see themselves as facing a rapidly deteriorating situation. As we saw in Chapter 2, their unsponsored-care costs (care provided without payment by or on behalf of the patient minus state and local government subsidies and grants), plus a shortfall gap between reimbursements and costs for treating Medicaid patients, have escalated sharply in recent years. Because there cannot be any truly uncompensated costs (in a market system, somebody pays for all resources used), what the hospitals cannot collect from some patients gets cost-shifted onto other insured parties and their payers, eventuating in higher premiums for everyone.

Beyond the institutional payers and the providers seeking payment, individual patients themselves constitute a group with a special awareness of one other cost category: prescription medications. Many who are reasonably covered for hospitalization and physician services are still at substantial financial and access risk when it comes to drugs. Clozaril, a drug used for schizophrenia, was priced at about $4,200 a year as of 1990. AZT, an antiviral drug approved for AIDS treatment, costs about $3,000 annually. Ceredase—approved in early 1991 for treating a debilitating genetic disorder called Gaucher's disease—is the newest shocker: Its price began at *$200,000* for a year's dosage.

Although the elderly account for 30 percent of prescriptions, these are only covered by Medicare when one is hospitalized. Nor are they covered in some private plans. Although medications account for only 7 percent of total health costs, patients face a far greater burden than that fact alone would suggest because they pay out-of-pocket for three-fourths of the $45 billion annual cost.

What Kind of Results Do We Get for Our High Costs?

If our greater costs made our system more effective, then there would be no reason why we should not, as a wealthier nation, spend more per capita. However, when we look at infant mortality and life expectancy—rough but generally accepted measures for comparing health systems across nations—we find ourselves far from a leadership position. Our 1988 life expectancy of 71.5 years for males compares with 73.0 in Canada, 75.5 in Japan, and 72.4 in the United Kingdom. In infant mortality, despite a welcome reduction to 9.1 deaths per 1,000 live births in 1990, we continue to rank below more than a dozen other nations, with Japan doing the best at 5.0 even though it spends less than half as much per person on health care than does the United States.

Both the health and the sickness of our system are captured in two facts: Half the 1990 improvement in infant-mortality rates is attributable to technological development—two new drugs used to prevent sudden respiratory failure in premature infants; and we fail to provide ordinary, "low-tech" prenatal care to many thousands of pregnant women each year.

In another measure of child health, we have fallen back some distance in immunizations against infectious diseases, especially measles, as earlier noted. Comments on this situation by Dr. Donald A. Henderson, who chaired a National Vaccine Advisory Committee, succinctly illustrate that the high costs symptomatic of an ailing system coexist with ineffective results:

> Immunization is the simplest procedure in the entire medical armamentarium, and is by far the most cost effective of all the medical interventions we have. [Yet] we have a huge increase in deaths due to measles for the first time in two decades. We also think there is some acute deterioration of the health care system, and we fear that this may be a warning flag for other problems to come.[2]

We, the People, Expect Better Health Care

A widely reported set of public opinion polls was conducted in late 1988 to look at the level of public satisfaction with the health care available in three countries. In the United States, 89 percent thought "fundamental changes" or complete rebuilding was needed, but only 43 percent in Canada and 69 percent in Britain had such a view of their system. Clearly, we are dissatisfied with the status quo in some way.

When people were asked what kind of national program should be adopted to ensure that everyone has health care coverage (which three-fourths of the public sees as a "right" in almost all surveys), however, there was a substantial split between those favoring a universal public system and those who opted for mandated employee-benefit insurance supplemented by government insurance for those not employed.

Business leaders seem to be as frustrated about the health care situation as is the general public. In October 1989, all members of Congress received a joint plea for help from the National Association of Manufacturers, the U.S. Chamber of Commerce, the National Federation of Independent Businesses, and the National Association of Wholesaler-Distributors. Saying that the viability of our health care system was threatened by leaping costs, the group letter called for cooperative government-business action (not further defined, however) to improve quality, phase in access for the uninsured, and control costs. A 1991 survey of CEOs in *Fortune*-list companies also found a high degree of dissatisfaction—and an equally high degree of ambivalence about what kind of governmental action would be justified. For example, according to this Robert Wood Johnson Foundation–sponsored study,

- Ninety-one percent thought "fundamental changes" were needed, and over half agreed that some government intervention would be needed;
- More than three-quarters thought government should provide tax incentives to encourage small firms to offer health insurance, but nearly as many would not *require* employers to provide health benefits;
- Forty percent supported expansion of existing public programs to cover more of the uninsured, and 28 percent favored regulating payments to doctors and hospitals, yet not even 10 percent supported replacing what we have now with a public health insurance system for all Americans (although one-fourth thought that a public-sector step should be considered for the future).

Although these and many similar findings are ambivalent—reflecting different question formats and contexts—and provide no clear path to an acceptable solution, they do demonstrate very substantial unhappiness with what we have now. Because patient satisfaction is increasingly being used as a measure of the quality of health care, these combined signs of discontent and disagreement about what to do may be taken as yet another symptom of serious illness, as defined by the public for whom the system is presumptively designed.

We Americans hold high expectations of what doctors and hospitals can do for us. Exactly because we recognize great strengths in American health care, we take as symptomatic of serious institutional weakness our failure to make even ordinary care available with dignity to all of our people at a cost acceptable either individually or institutionally.

4
What's Causing the Problems?

We turn now to the "why" questions: Why are so many uninsured or underinsured? Why is our system, despite its failure to cover everyone, the most expensive in the world?

How a Market System Works:
No Insurance, No Access

The explanation for uneven access to health care involves a host of factors. Among them are the resurgence since the early 1980s of devil-take-the-hindmost individualism as the dominant social attitude; our action-inhibiting political pluralism and program fragmentation; an emphasis in insurance programs on curative efforts with some disincentive to use preventive measures; a professional ethic in the American medical community (reinforced by the attitudes of well-insured patients) that gives higher priority to being on the cutting edge rather than to seeing that no one goes without needed primary care; a related thirst for procedural innovation that may add $12 billion a year to costs; and changes in health care financing patterns that are increasingly replacing the traditional means of minimizing inequity in access with destabilizing cost-containment policies.

Public-sector programs are supposed to assure access for those otherwise uninsured but obstacles remain. The architecture of Medicaid allows states to make wildly variant eligibility and coverage decisions. Changes in patterns of care, such as the increasing need for long-term care for elderly patients with chronic diseases, have decreased the effective coverage of Medicare.

Without covering everything, let's concentrate on the most fundamental of access-inhibiting causes: the misplaced application of market competition doctrines in a funding approach that treats health care as if it were just another optional consumer good.

In Chapter 2, I described U.S. health care as mostly private, financially speaking. In economists' terms, health care is predominantly provided on a market basis. More bluntly put, that means no money, no services, for the very essence of a market approach is an exchange of money. Economic "demand" is not what it sounds like: It is not just that I want something, no matter how strongly; demand is desire *plus enough money to pay the price set by the seller.*

The inadequacy of the market way of distributing health care is hidden from us to the extent that we enjoy third-party payer coverage, that is, our employer is picking up the tab for most or all of our medical expenses. So let's strip away that fortuitous circumstance and look at a scenario in which we really are buying health care on the same basis that we buy a VCR or a dinner out, or even a week's supply of groceries.

If a dog bit me, I might get to the nearest urgent care center (free-standing minor emergency facilities, sometimes referred to as a Doc in a Box), get a shot, and have an antiseptic applied—and pay cash or put the charges on my personal credit card. Treatment would cost perhaps $35–$100, bearable for most middle-class persons, though not what many families would want added unexpectedly to their week's purchases.

This unpredictability of need is one of several ways in which health care is different, and the unpredictability involves both timing and treatment. Illness is democratic in this respect—it can strike anyone. Furthermore, the purchase in the situation presented is not optional or deferrable: The services are needed, not just wanted, and treatment must be immediate. The VCR I want is a discretionary purchase. The treatment of an animal bite—or of the flu or a heart attack or a broken leg—is not. And we really don't decide for ourselves what we "want": A conventional estimate holds that physicians acting as their patients' agents make the decisions accounting for 70 percent or more of the nation's health care costs.

If the need is for a bypass operation or brain surgery, or even for a magnetic resonance imaging (MRI) examination to determine just what is needed, the cost may range from a thousand dollars for the test to over a hundred thousand for the procedure. In the absence of insurance, the true social cost of supplying health care on a market basis would come home to almost anyone at that point. The selection of patients to receive organ transplants provides a good case in point. Eighty-seven percent of transplant surgeons responding to a survey said that ability to pay was a very major consideration in selection of recipients. That's a good part of what we mean by "catastrophic" illness: A financial catastrophe is the price we pay for avoiding a medical catastrophe.

Another difference in buying health care is that one often cannot ascertain the total cost of the "product" before purchasing it. Although Medicare is instituting a fee schedule for physician services, it cannot dictate which and how many services will be needed.

Suppose you have unusual abdominal pains accompanied by headaches—a combination probably not diagnosable just by stethoscopic examination and conversation. First you ask the doctor what services will be needed. She may have to do tests before she can answer your question. The first test may lead to a second, but the doctor cannot predict that in advance. And the full treatment needed cannot be determined until all the diagnostic steps have been completed. Suppose you get to that point and the physician is then able to provide a price estimate. Unlike shopping for VCRs, in this case you've incurred substantial costs for deciding what you "want" by the time you learn the price. If you don't like (or can't afford) the price of treatment, are you likely to repeat this process with another physician picked out of the yellow pages, paying for a second diagnosis and estimate? Not likely.

And let's not forget that health care is also different in that it can be a matter of life or death and is almost always a matter of at least serious concern because our ability to function normally as workers or family members depends on good health. Quality (more accurately, reputation for quality, because we generally lack either direct evidence or seals of approval beyond that provided by a license to practice) is more important than price when it comes to health care. In buying a VCR, one might purposely choose the lower-quality model because it is cheaper. In health care quality, few of us would voluntarily make that choice. Clearly most household budgets could not accommodate the erratic, sometimes huge, expenses that modern health care often involves. Indeed, major medical miracles often carry a price tag that would wipe out whatever savings most families have as backup funds for emergencies, Americans being very poor savers on the whole.

In this scenario of individual responsibility for medical bills, the equity of health care distribution would necessarily mirror the equity (or inequity) of income distribution in the society. Because the United States has the most *un*equal distribution of income among industrial nations (its top-to-bottom family income ratio was 12 to 1 in the early 1980s; that of Canada was 9 to 1, West Germany 5 to 1, and Japan 4 to 1—and the top fifth's position even improved between 1980 and 1990), health care distributed entirely according to individuals' ability to pay would be *very* inequitable. In a pure market system, many would simply go without care. Charity and "uncompensated care" would fill the gap only when needed for a very small proportion of a provider's clientele.

What saves most of us as individuals—and saves the system from total collapse—is the fact that our actual system is not primarily characterized by individual purchases in a private market but by what can most accurately be called "private collectivism." For that is what the employer-sponsored health insurance system truly is. Sixty-six percent of all Americans have their primary health coverage through employer-sponsored plans, and 92 percent of employees in medium and large firms are so insured, with the firms paying most of the costs. If we had to buy this insurance individually—at $200–$300 a month, or even more without the advantage of group rates—far fewer of us would be covered. The company, government agency, school system, or nonprofit organization we work for acts as a nongovernmental collective that finances and supplies health insurance.

Middle- and upper-income people don't often recognize their dependence on someone else to pay the bulk of their medical bills. When asked if they pay their own way for doctor and hospital bills—in contrast to those whose care is paid for out of charity or Medicaid—a majority unthinkingly say yes. Blinded by our own individualistic rhetoric, we forget the third-party payer's predominant role and how small, relatively, is our personal financial role as "copayer." In fact, most of us would be uninsured and seeking government help if it were not for the private collectivism of employee-benefit health coverage. We of the middle- and upper-income groups may (should) be able to handle smaller health care expenses individually; but we would generally be in no better position to handle major medical or hospital bills on our own than are the poor and uninsured we too often tend to look down upon as lacking self-reliance. We're just luckier in our choice of employers. Health care is treated very much as a market good in the United States, but luckily for most of us, it is the organizations we work for that have to purchase it, not ourselves as individuals.

Both large and small firms are being affected by a rule of the Financial Accounting Standards Board that requires company balance sheets, beginning in 1993, to recognize the financial liabilities implicit in future medical benefits for retirees. The aggregate obligation is estimated at $335 billion. Having to include those previously unlisted obligations in financial statements will unfortunately tempt firms to reduce coverage to make the balance sheet look better. This is not likely to affect current employees, but future hires will probably not find as favorable a health benefit package.

At present, it is those who work in small firms or low-wage industries who are most likely to face the realities of the market approach to health care finance. And there are some further ironies in the employer-based system. For one, the uninsured low-wage worker helps subsidize the very full coverage of the insured high-wage worker every time he buys whatever is produced by the latter—an automobile, for instance, whose price includes several hundred dollars of corporate health care expenditure. For another, the tax exemption of fringe-benefit insurance gives greater financial relief to the higher-tax-bracket employee than to the lower one, though the latter needs the dollars more. In short, our reliance on tax-advantaged employee-benefit health insurance as our primary vehicle for health care finance creates great access inequities. These access inequities not only reinforce accurate perceptions of other inequities in our economic system but lead to further hardships among the disadvantaged.

Use of market approaches does not stop with how we get insured. It continues in the efforts of employers to stem their cost increases and in the competition of insurers to get corporate contracts. We have seen the impact of these dynamics in the symptoms of cost containment by means of increased employee cost-sharing through copremiums, deductibles, and copayments, as well as decreased benefits or reduced coverage for dependents and retirees. Cost-sharing does indeed reduce utilization, hence costs, but has the side effect noted earlier of reducing needed care as well as some that is not needed. Most appalling, cost-sharing deters access most of all for poor children according to data from the RAND Health Insurance

Experiment. Access for those in greatest need is therefore far from assured even when they have some insurance.

Health insurers competing for corporate contracts have moved away from community rating to experience rating and have recently been pushing so far that the very concept of insurance as a pooling of risk is being lost. Rates may be set for small firms on the basis of close examination of the health records of each individual to be covered and may even exclude some individual employees entirely. Increasingly, too, as insurers insert into employer contracts clauses excluding for a year—or sometimes indefinitely—new employees and their dependents who have histories of high blood pressure, diabetes, heart disease, or cancer, more and more people face a choice of "going bare" (i.e., without insurance) or facing "job lock" because of their medical histories. So health care access becomes problematic for some of those in the executive suites, not just for those dishing out fast food. "Cream-skimming" (avoiding subscribers most likely to become patients) charges have been made by insurance critics for several years, but the new aggressiveness in avoiding potentially risky patients is producing a residue for millions about as tasty as skim milk in comparison.

Another deterrent to provider willingness to care for under- and uninsured patients lies in the combined effect of insurer competition and employer cost-containment demands. In the case of hospitals, this combination means that payers are no longer willing to accept the charges claimed by the providers if those include some share of the uncompensated costs for care of other patients. (We should note the national government's unwillingness—despite its constitutional obligation for the general welfare—to take a communitywide view of its obligations as Medicare payer. It, too, insists on paying no share of uncompensated costs—ironically pushing the private sector ever closer to throwing in the towel and resigning itself to universal public health care financing that would vastly increase government's obligations.) In the case of physicians, the combination of insurer competition and employer cost containment means that fees are often challenged and doctors feel compelled to agree to cut-rate reimbursement by joining PPOs. In both cases, the traditional cross-subsidy arrangement by which the whole community shared in the costs of care for those who could not afford it on their own has been severely eroded, and with it the willingness or ability of providers to deliver the same care for all, regardless of income. Two other trends during the past decade have exacerbated this situation: Philanthropic gifts to hospitals have declined because donors assumed that the spread of insurance and government payments had lessened the need for charitable dollars; and larger corporations have moved toward self-insurance (setting aside their own funds from which to pay claims, usually hiring an insurance company to administer the program). From 1982 to 1988 the number of workers in self-insured plans rose from 5 million to over 11 million, and the number is almost certainly larger in 1992, especially as smaller firms are hopping on the bandwagon in order to contain costs.

Self-insurance usually carries with it the cost-containing policy of not accepting full charges from providers (thus escaping having to share in the communitywide burden). But its major way of saving money—to the detriment of employees—is by a legal quirk that allows a company's coverage to be less complete (often leaving out drug and alcohol rehabilitation and sometimes mental health treatment) than that which an insurance company might be required to offer under state-legislated mandates. In effect, by avoiding state mandates, self-insuring firms completely control the design of their plans, and the state insurance commissions cannot insist on inclusions deemed good from a public policy perspective. Thus the completeness of insurance-funded access is further reduced, even for the employed insured.

Another access consequence of these market-oriented retrenchments in health care finance is that the more successful the effort of large companies to shift costs away from themselves, the less able insurers are to offer small companies affordable rates without very heavy cost-sharing by the employees. Cost-shifting also is a major cause of increases in indemnity insurance premiums, which further diminishes the availability of coverage and increases the cost barrier for employees. One analysis identifies cost-shifting as the cause of one-third of premium increases in 1987–1988.

Note the ironic reversal in health care finance: Before insurance was widely available, cross subsidy was for many years an effective way of spreading medical care risks by shifting costs to those who could afford more than actual cost from those who could not afford full costs. Community rating as the basis for insurance premiums supported cross subsidy when it might otherwise have become too burdensome for individual providers to handle simply by a sliding scale of fees. But now the pressures of employment-based competition and self-interested cost containment have turned cost-shifting on its head and forced the higher costs onto those *least* able to bear them: small firms, individuals buying nongroup policies, and the less healthy members of indemnity plans.

Competition of course means attention to costs: The insurance firm with lower costs can set the most attractive price for consumers. But greater efficiency is not the only (and probably not the easiest) route to lower costs. Marketing strategies aimed at selection of the healthiest persons is another approach to lower costs, but one that can purposely impede access for less healthy persons. An HMO may establish its clinics in upper-income suburban areas or hold a supposedly open-to-all-seniors recruitment meeting by offering a third-floor dance, which only the hardier potential clients will reach.

Cost containment in the form of offering strong incentives for employees to join HMOs further reduces access in the sense that full access traditionally meant free choice of provider. In a very large HMO, especially one of those that also offers a supplementary preferred-provider list, this restriction may not be much noticed. But for those older employees who have long enjoyed a relationship with a physician who happens not to be in the HMO, either one's access is diminished or one accepts the hurdle of paying more as the price of continued free choice.

We should also note a public-sector "market" dimension, one that undercuts Medicaid's effectiveness. Physician participation rates have been decreasing as state-regulated fees fall behind charges accepted by other payers. Medicaid can't even compete with Medicare for a doctor's services: Medicaid pays, on average, 69 percent of what Medicare pays, and, of course, in comparison with private insurer reimbursement pays even less. An apparent trade-off has been occurring: As Congress mandates that states cover a larger proportion of the poor in their Medicaid programs, some states are making up for the added expenses by decreasing the fee per visit or per procedure. What the right hand giveth in eligibility the left hand taketh away in cost containment!

Why Do Costs Rise So Much, So Fast?

Knowing that health care cost inflation leads the pack doesn't tell us what the components are of this unprecedented, unwanted, and ever-increasing growth in claims on the nation's dollars. Let's quickly sketch the broad picture and then look more closely at some specifics.

General inflation—cost increases that medical providers share with the economy at large, from building costs for a hospital to the cleaning supplies used in it every day—accounts for about half of each year's total rise in health care costs, leaving the other half to be accounted for by factors specific to this "industry." It is this other half that makes health care's inflation rate far greater than if it simply matched the consumer price index (CPI).

Prices in the Health Care "Market Basket"

A substantial chunk of this second half, perhaps over 20 percent, lies in the price increases specific to health care. One part of this consists of higher prices for the "market basket" of products—from tongue depressors, bed pans, and syringes to the measuring devices, instrumentation panels, wires, and tubes of an intensive care unit (ICU). A second part reflects the expansion of what is in the market basket: home health care, for example, which began as a cost-reducing alternative to hospital care but whose spread may well end up adding to total costs. Yet another component of health-specific inflation is higher incomes for doctors, nurses, and even hospital orderlies.

Health care is a labor-intensive industry, so rising personnel costs have a greater impact than in more equipment-oriented businesses such as those dealing in electric power generation and distribution. Some health care personnel were for decades badly underpaid by any standard; only now are their salaries being brought to appropriate levels. Nurses, for example, are one health care resource in short supply and are at last beginning to receive salaries appropriate to their increasing professional responsibilities. Nurses' aides, too, are only now starting to earn beyond the minimum wage. Physician incomes, however, rose by 8.1 percent annually in 1977–1987 compared with 5.5 percent for other nonfarm workers. In 1989, median doctor income rose 12.8 percent, three times the rate of inflation.

Much of our success in warding off death and curing illnesses involves very expensive technologies and complex procedures requiring equipment-filled facilities and hordes of "allied health care" professionals and technicians to operate and monitor the equipment. The doctor and the patient are still there, but a lot more than a stethoscope comes between them today.

In more professional language, the intensity of care (which includes the services supplied and the underlying equipment and facilities) is rising at a rapid rate and may explain roughly a fourth of the increase in health care costs. The technological element is crucial, in itself and in its multifarious ramifications, and we will examine it in detail in this chapter.

The relative shares of these major categories of cost-causing factors varies year by year, but perhaps typical of recent years are the 1988 data. These showed that year's increased costs as due to general price inflation, 43 percent; medical-sector price inflation, 24 percent; population changes, 10 percent; and "all other factors" (with technology a major component), 23 percent. If we take away general inflation to reveal real increases, then technology and health-specific price increases may each amount to about half the total, with the structure and incentives of the payment system a major factor underlying expansion of costs in both the health care market basket and technology-intensive spheres.

Before taking a closer look at the causative roles of the payment system and advancing technology in cost escalation, let's look briefly at some of the other contributing factors:

• We have an increasingly large and increasingly elderly population (the over-65 group was 32 million in 1990 and will reach about 36 million by 2000; the over-85 cohort was 3.3 million in 1990 and will be 6 million by 2010), and use of health care increases with age. Thirty percent of hospital expenses and of prescription drug costs are for the 10 percent who are 65 or older.

• Use of diagnostic and therapeutic equipment is spreading to nonhospital settings like urgent care centers, and even individual physician's offices. This increases the number of units of equipment that have to be paid for by using them on patients whenever plausibly justified.

• The human cost of the escalating AIDS epidemic (43,000 cases reported in 1990 and, cumulatively, 500,000–800,000 Americans infected) is accompanied by financial costs that are anticipated to reach $10.8 billion in 1994, from $5.8 billion in 1991.

• The United States has a higher ratio of specialists to primary-care doctors than almost any other country, with each specialist quite naturally inclined to use his skills.

• The customary physician payment structure encourages expensive technical procedures and surgery because reimbursements for these procedures are far more generous than for what is called "cognitive medicine" (taking a patient's history, doing a diagnosis with an emphasis on the doctor's skills and judgment rather more than on lab tests, and treating conditions with medication rather than technological procedures when there is a choice of approach).

• The administrative costs of a private-sector, and partially profit-oriented, health care system are far greater than those of a single-payer public system. One recent estimate puts 1987 administrative costs in the United States at about 20 percent of health care expenditures, having risen 37 percent in just four years. For Canada, the estimated comparable figure was only half as much. Even if this analysis exaggerated the difference, as some critics charged, it is clear that a system with 1,500 different insurance programs will have more complicated paperwork than one with a single payer. And that's apart from the marketing expenses that are entirely absent in Canada but increasing in the United States as competition increases among large-scale providers and insurers. Institutional fragmentation has its price.

• And let's not forget malpractice suits and defensive medicine. The contention is that punitive damage awards lead to higher insurance premiums for doctors, so they are encouraged to do much more testing than may be medically warranted in order to defend themselves from malpractice claims.

A much longer book than this one—indeed, a number of books—would be needed to examine all of these factors in detail. Here we concentrate most of our attention on two: technology and the payment system.

High-Tech: Its Use, Abuse, and Costs

"Medical Technology 'Arms Race' Adds Billions to the Nation's Bill," runs a *New York Times* headline (April 29, 1991) for an article examining the expensive diffusion now going on of the newest imaging machine, a positron emission tomography (PET) scanner. CAT (computer-assisted tomography) and MRI imaging provide cross-sectional data on tissue structures; PET scanners reveal information on tissue functioning and biochemical processes as well, giving them a clear place of value in the armamentarium of noninvasive diagnostic instruments. One cost-effective example: At a testing cost of perhaps $2,000 it is possible to determine whether a coronary bypass operation is worth doing at $30,000.

Cost-effective use, however, comes after very considerable capital investment and may be accompanied by some very cost-*in*effective utilization as well. PET scanners may cost $3.6–$4.2 million compared with $1.2–$2.5 million for the MRI and $400,000–$1.2 million for the CAT. And the capital investment is only the beginning of what these machines will add to the health care bill. It's their daily use that runs up the bill. Typical fees for using the imaging machines compare this way: CAT-scan, $300–$500; MRI-scan, $600–$1,000; PET-scan, $1,500–$2,000. Cumulatively, the addition to national health expenditures is enormous—on the MRI alone, a cost approaching $5 billion in 1990 for some 5 million scans done on the 2,000 MRIs now on line.

There is no doubt that each of these imagers adds to the quality of health care in some cases. There *is* doubt that we need as many such machines as we have or that we need to use them as often as we do. In the case of CAT and MRI, the water has already passed over the dam—4,900 CAT scanners and 1,990 MRI machines were in place by 1991. (On a per capita basis, we have four times as many MRIs as Germany and eight times as many as Canada.) But there were only 50 PET scanners in place, and a number of observers, both medically and financially motivated, are hoping to keep their proliferation down, as Andrew Pollack reports in the *Times* article. If the number of machines is limited, there will be less investment-recovering pressure to use them beyond the point at which the costs might exceed the potential benefit. Restricting the number of machines will be an uphill battle, as the MRI's history makes clear.

The MRI was introduced in the mid-1980s and use spread ("diffused" is the health care industry term) with great speed, with no organized effort on the part of insurance companies, corporate payers, or the government to establish guidelines for how many would be needed or medical indicators for when use of MRI made sense.

Unlike the majority of hospitals, the manufacturers of medical devices are all in the for-profit sector of the economy (General Electric is the leading producer of MRIs) and quite appropriately have the bottom line in mind when they try to sell as many units as possible. Hospitals become easy sales targets as they compete with one another for patients by attracting physicians, and they attract physicians partly by having the latest equipment available in the "doctors' workshop." When one hospital got an MRI, others in the same community felt a need to jump on the bandwagon.

Outside of hospitals, medical entrepreneurs—and there are many in an $800 billion industry—saw an opportunity to make money by setting up free-standing imaging centers; and they often solicited physicians (who could refer patients) as co-owners. Once the machines are sitting there, the incentives to use them to the maximum are strong indeed: The owners want to recoup their investment and the physicians want the extra degree of diagnostic certainty that imaging tests can sometimes provide. But conflicts of interest arise when the owners and the using physicians are overlapping persons, giving extra incentives to call for tests and to specify where they will be performed. A later story (*New York Times*, June 2, 1991) found that in Florida three-fourths of the imaging centers were owned or partly owned by physicians and Atlanta, Georgia's 30 MRI centers were mostly owned by the same doctors that ordered the tests. The connection between ownership and referrals is explicit in prospectuses for limited partnerships being established to finance imaging centers, the *Times* story noted.

In short, technology is not a product of spontaneous generation; strong market forces impel its use.

But all the blame does not lie with the manufacturers and the health care providers. We as patients also play a role. As Professor John Caronna of Cornell Medical Center says, "There's no way to shut it off. The doctors crave it, it's reassuring, and the patients crave it" (well-insured patients, presumably, who like to feel that their care is given in the latest style).

Trying to avoid overutilization of existing machines and overdiffusion of new ones like PET scanners is hard because there are many incentives to go ahead, but few stop signs—so far. (Medicare regulations may soon slow down the tendency to rush into the new technologies, however, as discussed in Chapter 6.)

The imagers are one of the more expensive examples of how new technologies are introduced, spread, and perhaps overutilized without careful weighing of costs relative to advantages, but they are far from unique in this respect. Another strong example is that of TPA (tissue plasminogen activator), an anticlotting drug used in transplant operations. Despite a price *ten times* that of the drug it substitutes for, streptokinase, it came into widespread use very quickly, with many physicians convinced (perhaps as much by manufacturer promotional efforts as by solid evidence) that it was superior. After several years of patients or insurers paying $2,200 instead of $200, research reported in major journals in 1991 showed not only that TPA did not work better but that it was actually *less safe*.

Technology Is Procedures and Spare Parts, Too

Technology is not just equipment or machinery. It includes specific ways of doing things, too: "procedures." And these can vary tremendously in cost, with the new sometimes more and sometimes less expensive than the old. For clogged arteries around the heart, for example, there is the surgical approach of a bypass operation or the much less invasive procedure of angioplasty, which means inserting a tube into the artery and stretching it by expanding a balloon at the narrowed points. Both approaches are expensive, but the bypass costs more. Some experts contend that both are overused, which often means used on patients for whom the likelihood of benefit is very slim indeed. Dr. Robert H. Brook of UCLA and RAND has expressed the belief that from a third to a half of what we do is of such little benefit that insurance should not pay for it. One reason for such overuse is the lack of guidelines a doctor can rely on to determine appropriate use of technology—which means that the charge of overutilization might be as meaningful as Monday morning quarterbacking. Overuse also occurs because doctors practice defensive medicine (itself stimulated by medical uncertainty) in order to minimize malpractice suits, insurance companies are willing to cover these therapies (fewer uninsured patients have these performed), and the payment system rewards procedures over the prescribing of medications. Sometimes, too, providers may rationalize a need in order, for example, to keep a hospital heart operations team (surgeons, specialized nurses, anesthesiologists, and assorted technicians) busy—which is important both economically and in order to keep skills well honed.

In 1988, we were spending $5 billion annually on 200,000 bypass operations. Bypasses were one of five procedures that had only recently become routine yet were already being so widely used that each of the five accounted for at least $1 billion annually in costs. The other four were angioplasty, transurethral prostatectomy (a prostate operation also thought to be overused), hip operations, and gallbladder removals.

Another area of burgeoning technological invention—and burgeoning cost—is that of "replacement parts." As with cars, these often cost far more than did the "original equipment." Reporter Mike Schwartz ("Body by Man," Riverside, Calif., *Press-Enterprise,* April 9, 1991) cataloged 24 different artificial body parts now in use, ranging from the most common—artificial hip joints (200,000 a year implanted)—through intraocular lenses used in cataract cases to cardiac pacemakers and expandable thigh bone implants for children to allow for growth.

By far the most costly of these replacement parts is one not yet even in production: the permanent artificial heart. Research expenditures on it have already totaled almost a quarter billion dollars, yet it is years away from reaching a usable stage. In fact, the National Heart, Lung and Blood Institute tried to end its contracts for work on a fully implantable heart in favor of using the funds on the more promising left ventricular assist (a partial heart replacement). Politics intruded, however: Both Utah and Massachusetts have contracts, so the strange-bedfellows senatorial team of Orrin G. Hatch (R., Utah) and Edward M. Kennedy (D., Mass.) forced a resuscitation of the total replacement research funding. As far back as 1985, a study published by the institute estimated that the technology might cost (in 1983 dollars) $2.5 billion for development and then $5 billion annually for its use. While we wait for the artificial heart, over 1,600 transplants of real hearts are being done annually at an average 1989 cost of about $120,000.

It is not just the technologies themselves that increase costs. The rise of medical technology curiously increases rather than decreases the labor intensiveness of the health care industry, particularly for nurses and technology operators and monitors. The average hospital patient is sicker today and requires more care than ever before, and with more sophisticated equipment. Sicker patients and complicated equipment call for more hands-on attention, and that means more nurses. In 1972, there were 50 registered nurses per 100 hospital patients; by 1987 there were 97.8.

One final item in this very incomplete litany of technology-related causes of cost inflation is the greater willingness of patients to undergo major treatment procedures because many ailments can now be treated noninvasively and thus with less danger and far less body "downtime," thanks to technological advances. Physician Harvey J. Cohen pointed out the irony in a letter to *Business and Health* (April 1990): Although noninvasive diagnostic procedures may be individually less costly than exploratory surgery, the total cost, he wrote, "is considerably higher since so many more of them are being done compared to the invasive ones formerly performed."

Technological marvels and a cultural mind-set that encourages rushing to use each new piece of equipment or advance in technical procedures pervade the entire health care world, from basic research to bedside treatment of the patient. Ours is often called a "Do something" culture, but it is really more than that. The extended version found in medicine today is: "Don't just do something—do it in a high-tech way."

Probably the only safe statement one can make is that the geometric rate of increase in expensive technologies, both machines and procedures for using them, is a major—perhaps *the* major—cause of health care expense escalation. This increase rate is vastly exacerbating both the cost-containment debate and the access crisis, because the more valuable the miracles we can perform, the more troublesome become the financial barriers to access.

Payment Perversities and Moral Hazard

In what is known as the political economy of health care, financial incentives are said to contribute most to the exploding-cost pattern by encouraging expenditures beyond those medically indicated. The traditional pattern and current attempts to reverse incentives were covered briefly in Chapter 2. Here we look more closely at the implications of the aspect peculiarly called "moral hazard" in the jargon of insurance economics. At a microlevel—that of individual doctors, hospitals, patients—incentives to overutilize care are said to stem from a bundle of phenomena explainable in terms of these components:

- Payments to doctors on an FFS (fee-for-service) basis
- Payments to hospitals on the basis of charges for each and every service performed and the supplies and pieces of equipment used
- Payments to both on a retrospective basis, so that the total bill is knowable only after the services have been "purchased"

- The fact that much of reimbursement to providers is by "third-party payers"

If we put all these together, we have "moral hazard," which many economists seem to make into the black beast of the system. Because so much blame is placed on moral hazard, and because it is so often used as a justification for making patients pay higher out-of-pocket shares of health care expenses, it is worth shining a spotlight on.

Whose Moral Hazard?

Moral hazard refers to the risk (from the insurer's viewpoint) that people will have an incentive to use more health care than they need simply because someone else is paying for it. Among economists—because of the doctrinal assumption of their discipline that each of us acts to maximize individual financial gain—it has been tempting to see this consumer (= patient) incentive as a major, even *the* major, cause of health care cost escalation. It has been suggested, for example, that although fire insurance does not provide an incentive to commit arson because that would negate the coverage when discovered, health insurance consumers can seek to gain from their health insurance by using more health care. (A policy corollary considered in Chapter 6 says that cost escalation resulting from moral hazard can only be avoided if consumers are forced to share in the costs so that using more means a greater out-of-pocket loss to them.)

There is truth in the psychological assumption behind the moral hazard doctrine, but its effect is both overstated and misplaced as generally applied. First, the true element: If I have a runny nose and my body aches, I may have an ordinary head cold that antibiotics can do nothing to cure, or I may have the flu, against which medication can be effective. Without insurance (third-party payment), I'm likely to take two aspirin and see how I feel in the morning. With insurance, I might rush to my physician for a diagnosis and a prescription in case it turns out to be flu. Or if I am playing tennis or softball and twist an ankle, with insurance I might seek immediate treatment, including diagnostic x-rays for a possible fracture. Without it, I'm more likely to just hope it's a minor sprain, tape it up, and wait and see.

Everyone with good insurance will be susceptible to this kind of moral hazard incentive, especially if the coverage is "first dollar" (i.e., without any copayment) and if getting the care is convenient in time and place. Whether use of the insurance in these circumstances constitutes *over*use is hard to say; that is at least in part a matter of subjective judgment and individual circumstances.

However, I am no more likely to seek out a coronary bypass operation or delicate and very expensive brain surgery just because I am insured than I am to steer my car into a tree just because I have collision coverage. There is a natural limit on the incentive economists worry about and it lies in the fact that we do not have an incentive to pursue health care for its own sake. Purchasing health care is not a positive good in itself (except perhaps for some hypochondriacs) but an unfortunate necessity brought on by accident or disease. We want a nice car for its own sake; that's not true of a nice appendectomy scar. Canadian health economist Robert G. Evans has pointed out that a health insurance "beneficiary" is not someone to be envied for an economic gain but someone who is less fortunate than others because of having suffered from some medically insured illness. He suggests as an example spending two weeks in a resort versus two weeks in a hospital. Even though the hospital devotes more resources to the person's welfare, we envy the person who is in the first situation and hope not to be in the second. If we look at it this way, it is ridiculous to suppose that people have much of an incentive to overuse the health care system just because of third-party payment. (Incidentally, we are less likely to confuse this point if we think of people seeking health care as *patients* rather than as *consumers*; the medical context provides a more sensible analytic framework than the assumed motivations of Adam Smith's Economic Man.)

And that brings us to the second point, that the economists' concern with moral hazard is badly misplaced. It is not so much the patients as the doctors, hospitals, and other providers who have a strong incentive to take advantage of third-party payment. We have already pointed out that Medicare has in recent years adopted some forms of prospective payment in an effort to modify and even (in the case of hospitals) reverse traditional incentives. But those rules are for services to Medicare patients and have not yet been adopted by enough of the private sector to turn the dominant incentive system away from its traditional retrospective mode.

That mode is clearly of the "Do something" type, and what to do is primarily up to the provider, not the patient. Keep in mind that the primary choice made by the patient is to choose a doctor. Once that is done, the rest of the "purchasing" decisions in health care are primarily made by the physician acting as the patient's agent. Estimates of the proportion of therapeutic decisions made by doctors as agents range upward from 70 percent: what tests to do; what hospital to enter; what operation(s) to perform; how long to stay in the hospital; what rehabilitation services to prescribe; and how many follow-up office visits to track the patient's progress until a complete recovery is achieved.

In looking at the impact of the market system on access, we have already seen that uninsured patients are less likely than the insured to have certain major procedures performed on them. The other side of this is that the providers obviously feel freer to draw on the complete storehouse of available services for the patient whose "wallet biopsy" reveals an insurance card. Let us hasten to say that professional integrity will almost always prevent the performance of services only as an income-generating device.

Despite these qualifiers, we do have to acknowledge some real stimuli for moral hazard practices to develop among providers when the insurance provides good coverage. The doctor can ask for the additional test that will make the diagnosis 99 percent certain instead of just 95 percent. A procedure that is only possibly of benefit but that will definitely not harm the patient may be performed because the outside payer is there. The doctor may delay the patient's discharge from the hospital to permit an extra day's recuperation when insurance will cover it; when not, the doctor may release the patient sooner. (In this example, the patient also shares in the moral hazard—although it is the doctor's orders to which the hospital will respond.)

Quite apart from the moral hazard of physician as agent are the fears of malpractice suits that motivate doctors to overutilize health care resources when insurance makes it financially feasible to do so. Although the aggregate addition to health care costs directly attributable to high malpractice premiums and jury awards is often exaggerated, it is generally conceded that the *in*direct effects are substantial. These take the form of doctors practicing "defensive medicine," which means ordering extra tests and doing procedures that may be of marginal value to avoid later charges that one committed sins of omission that assertedly harmed the patient. These costs are far greater than the direct ones of jury awards. In 1991 the AMA estimated that malpractice insurance premiums may add $5.6 billion to patients' bills and that about $15 billion is spent annually on defensive medicine.

Despite headlines about million-dollar jury awards, a major study published in 1990 (covering 1984 data) showed that only one lawsuit was filed for every 10 cases of medical negligence; that plaintiffs lose a majority of the cases; and that a jury awards damages in only 20 percent of the cases that go to trial. Insurance premiums for doctors make headlines when they rise rapidly but less so when they go down, as began to happen in 1990. This welcome cost decline reportedly results in part from a better kind of defensive medicine: use of monitoring devices to prevent deaths from anesthesiology errors and training of doctors to minimize the risk of errors in the types of cases most likely to result in lawsuits. Another reason is statutory: state laws that penalize frivolous claims, making attorneys more selective in cases they are willing to file.

Hospitals have similar incentives to encourage defensive medicine and overuse of procedures when the patient is covered by insurance. Administrators will not badger physicians to release, or transfer to public hospitals, well-insured patients with indemnity coverage that pays retrospectively. Hospital boards will, with the aid of sophisticated computerized cost analysis, seek to establish special "niche" programs that are especially well reimbursed by insurance programs: "profit centers" like psychiatric units, substance abuse programs, and sports rehabilitation clinics. The promotion of such facilities in both print ads and broadcast commercials suggests that people with any possibly appropriate symptoms for one or another of these types of care will be encouraged to utilize them. Does such encouragement produce some unneeded costs attributable to provider-induced moral hazard? Probably so. On the other side of the coin, hospitals do *not* compete these days to establish emergency rooms and maternity wards, both of which are likely to be loss centers. In fact, the business strategy of for-profit hospital chains sometimes calls for purposeful omission of these latter services.

Thus we see that moral hazard operates more strongly on the provider side than among patients. Providers have the leverage to call upon the system's resources, and they are generally and increasingly well aware of how to "press the buttons" of the insurance system. Those who supply the services can, in short, manipulate the demand side as well—within the boundaries of medical uncertainty that can justify extra measures on one side, and professional integrity that limits what one does on the other side. Although incentive-system reforms are impinging on this picture, it remains the dominant one as of 1992.

How Much Does Moral Hazard Push Up Costs?

The evidence on moral hazard's contribution to the cost crisis is not definitive because the uncertainties of medicine leave ample room for diverse judgments regarding what is necessary or unnecessary care. But we can draw two likely generalizations: Moral hazard is a significant if immeasurable factor, and its effect on costs should be laid far more at the feet of providers than of patients. The largely mistaken tendency to stress incentives for the patients to overutilize because of insurance payments really constitutes a case of blaming the victim.

We should add that if moral hazard were as big a factor as is sometimes supposed, costs should have headed downward by now because of the spread of utilization review (UR), including prehospitalization authorization and denial of excessive claims by doctors. The intrusive UR now practiced both in government programs and by private insurers makes it very difficult for patients or providers to succumb to moral hazard temptations even if they wanted to. Yet costs keep going up. Thus other factors are almost certainly far more significant. Further, this assessment is supported by other kinds of comparative information, for example, Canada offers first-dollar coverage, which should maximize the temptation, yet its health care utilization rates are no worse than in the United States and its costs are far lower per capita.

The Changing Picture of Incentives

Even apart from the specific incentive problem of moral hazard, the traditional provider incentives of our system have clearly reinforced the "Do something" ethic. The fee-for-service system is often cited as one of the major cost escalators, but that is not really true. FFS only became a problem as the rise of insurance coverage removed a financial obstacle that had earlier been an ordinary inhibiting factor in a physician's choices about testing and treatment. Until then, the flexibility of FFS was actually an important positive element in providing access through the doctor's use of "freedom of fees," so to speak, in order to cross-subsidize between well-off patients and charity cases. With insurance, and as long as the fees were simply whatever the physician wanted them to be (and the payer learned their level only after the services had been rendered), FFS did unquestionably become a major factor in raising costs. Similarly, hospital payments traditionally made on the basis of what the hospital chose to charge (without analysis of its actual costs in providing the care) and known only retrospectively became a very major cost-raising factor as insurance coverage developed.

So it was the *interaction* of FFS, third-party payment, and the retrospective and unilateral setting of the charges by the providers that became such a threat to containing health care costs—not FFS or third-party coverage by itself. In fact, of this bundle of factors pushing up costs, the more fundamental one is the after-the-fact dimension. That the incentive pattern needed reforming to reduce overuse beyond what was medically required was understood analytically as early as 1965 when Medicare and Medicaid were enacted. But the legislation and implementing regulations for Medicare ignored the opportunity for modifying the payment system. The reason, as Judith M. Feder effectively demonstrated in her 1977 book *Medicare: The Politics of Federal Hospital Insurance*, was that the "primary objective" was to see that the program got off to a good start, and the cooperation of providers was not to be risked.

This deference to providers' financial interests is what is now being changed by the growth of various forms of prospective payment—from the HMOs that now provide coverage and care for 36 million people to DRGs, hospital per diems, and volume performance standards, which are discussed and evaluated further in Chapter 6.

Now we have one more cause of our cost crisis to consider: the lack of central levers of budgetary control.

Where Are the Levers of Budgetary Control?

If we move our consideration from the microlevel of individual patients and providers to the macrolevel and look at the financial incentives of the system as a whole, we see that policy pluralism and program fragmentation have kept us from placing an overall cap on health care expenditures. The absence of an overall budgetary control in the United States constitutes a tremendous hole in the dike of cost containment, for in the absence of an expenditure ceiling, the tendency is to make technological discoveries additive rather than substitutive, as well as to make it extremely difficult to set aggregate limits on provider reimbursements.

Our total medical financial system is open-ended in a way that those of such other nations as Canada, Britain, and Germany are not. They use what is known as "global budgeting" to set an overall limit on a hospital, a region of the country, and sometimes on the whole country's expenditure in a particular category. We will look more closely at how global budgeting works—and the probable limits on its applicability for us—in Chapter 7. The essential point here is simply that if a single payer (e.g., a Canadian province) sets a fixed sum for a given year as what it will spend on health care, and on that basis lets hospitals and doctors know in advance what the limits will be on the reimbursement they can obtain, then those who "deliver" health care have a very strong incentive to exercise prudent judgment. And policymakers have an instrument in the budget for establishing priorities in the system, for example, by assuring primary care for all by making people wait for elective surgery or by seeing that all children are immunized as opposed to spending the same money on more MRI machines.

Without global budgeting a system has no overall cost controls and therefore is vulnerable to pressures from every quarter to add services to the mix while ignoring the cumulative impact on the budget.

The United States clearly suffers from such vulnerability. We have 1,500 insurers, retrospective reimbursement is still the dominant mode of payment, and open-ended government programs operate on the basis of largely unconstrained individual entitlements. Effective assessment of new technologies before they are widely dispersed is largely lacking. We are about at the opposite end of the budgetary spectrum from a country like Britain where the national government can effectively set a limit on health care expenditures covering 90 percent of the total care delivered.

Although this gloomy appraisal accurately reflects our present situation, there are some developing exceptions that constitute partial- or quasi-global budgeting, explained and evaluated in Chapter 7.

It remains to be seen how we will pursue the tremendously difficult political matter of incentive reforms at the macrolevel. As of 1992 the fragmented programs of our pluralistic health policy framework remain a major cause of runaway health care costs, regardless of what we may be able to accomplish at the individual level where the great bulk of cost-containment efforts have so far been focused.

Part Three

What Are the Options?

5
How Do We Get
Coverage for Everyone?

Every American should be assured of needed medical care, whether one sees care in terms of the individual's right to receive or in terms of society's obligation to provide. That is the principle underlying the analysis in this chapter. The question then becomes *How* can we best cure the "lack of coverage" disease that afflicts 34 million or more Americans?

A bewildering diversity of proposals has been offered in recent years, and nothing approaching a consensus has yet emerged. But the abundance of schemes can be limited to a range of types for description and analysis. This chapter includes a sketch of the types as well as the pros and cons and specific examples of each.[1]

Each proposal's scheme to impose cost discipline on the system will be briefly mentioned in this chapter and examined more extensively in the next two chapters. These examinations are a necessary prelude to the recommendations in the final chapter regarding the elements that would be found in an optimal program for combining universal access, cost control, and political feasibility.

The Red Herring of Socialized Medicine

The crux of the health care coverage reform debate turns on the appropriate mix of private and public elements. The critical questions are, Who pays for health care, and how? and, Who provides it?

As we have seen, the U.S. system is nearly unique in its private, market-oriented, employer-dominated financing, with thousands of different payers and plans—pluralism to the nth degree, one might say. The appropriateness of publicly financed health care is accepted for the elderly and (grudgingly) for the unemployed poor, but not for the bulk of the population. Our system is not unique, however, in its overwhelming use of the private sector to provide medical services. In fact, most Western nations combine public financing with private delivery of services. As we examine the range of alternatives, we need to keep in mind the ordinariness of this combination. It was purposely confused (with apparently lasting effect on public perceptions) in the AMA-sponsored public relations campaign that inaccurately portrayed President Truman's national health insurance (NHI) plan as "socialized medicine."

In the late 1940s that term was used to confuse government financing of health insurance with total government control of medical care and thus to conjure up the frightening prospect of Stalinist minions getting between you and your doctor. In fact, however, Truman's idea was to do for the entire population what Medicare has since done for the elderly: Take a major share of the health care financial burden off the shoulders of individual patients so that they could feel free to seek care as needed. As with Medicare, his NHI was designed to let the doctors remain fee-for-service individual practitioners and the hospitals remain totally in professional control. With the government paying the bills, doctors and hospitals would not need to provide as much charity care and sick people would not need to go without care or suffer the embarrassment of being charity cases.

In traditional social science usage, socialism means government ownership of the means of production. If we think of doctors and hospitals as the health care system's "means of production," then the Truman plan—or any other in which government's role is to pay private-sector providers on behalf of patients—is not "socialized medicine." Whether a government-*run* (as distinguished from -*financed*) health care system can be effective is, of course, debatable; but the socialized medicine charge sometimes revived today by opponents of any plan that is government financed is simply a red herring. It should not frighten us away from a dispassionate examination of the evidence concerning the more publicly oriented alternatives currently discussed.

The public-private mix can work in ways our ideological conventional wisdom may not lead us to expect. Consider the regulatory controls over professional decisions—such as insurance company requirements of clearance before a patient is hospitalized—that may occur in private-sector institutions. It is not just in governmental programs that a doctor may find administrators—private bureaucrats, some would say—looking over her shoulder. Conversely, a government-financed and partly government-owned system (e.g., the British National Health Service, which does own most hospitals) may leave decisions about the treatment given to individual patients largely to the professional judgment of the physicians because its overall budgetary controls make micromanagement unnecessary.

The Medicare program illustrates yet another possible combination. Originated on the basis that it would leave the practice of medicine alone, it has become quite intrusive with its DRGs, PROs, and RVSs. Yet the providers remain in the private sector and are not "socialized."

In short, whether the financing is predominantly private or public tells us little about incentives to provide or withhold care or about the extent to which the payer does or does not intervene between physician and patient. The most important considerations—medical effectiveness, equity, administrative and political feasibility, cost effectiveness, compatibility with patients' rights and physicians' professional responsibilities—cannot be settled by ideological sloganeering. We need to keep our minds open as we look at all the possibilities.

What Is the Range of Options?

Major congressional action on health care will be in the form of enacting a specific, detailed legislative plan and will doubtless include a number of compromises to bring powerful interests on board—just as was the case with Medicare and Medicaid. Yet whatever emerges will be recognizable as embodying predominantly one or another of a limited number of policy models or "ideal types."

At the most public end of the spectrum would be a national health service (NHS), in which the word "service" connotes government delivery of the services, as well as their financing. Next in degree of public-sector involvement are National Health Insurance (NHI) and Universal Health Insurance (UHI) systems.

NHI is primarily seen as a publicly (i.e., tax) financed insurance plan to cover the entire population, whether financed and operated by the national government or jointly by national and state governments. Extension of Medicare to the entire population is an example of an entirely national plan; Canada's system, with dual financing from the national government and the governments of the provinces, and operation at the provincial level, exemplifies the intergovernmental type. Another interpretation of NHI (but one that better fits UHI) is that an NHI is any health insurance system established by national law to cover the entire population that uses a mixture of public- and private-sector financing and operation. By terming this broader conception *Universal* Health Insurance, we can indicate the scope of coverage without necessarily implying governmental operation. Germany provides an example, as do the current play-or-pay proposals in the United States.

Using both terms would make public discussions more precise, with universal coverage the policy goal and national plans in the first sense being but one means. However, NHI is used at times in both senses, so one has to examine the details to see what is really meant.

Other broad types we'll look at include competitive managed care, employer mandates supplemented by adjustments to existing public coverage programs, and plans that represent incremental attempts to improve the private insurance system without much disturbing it (or its vested interests).

The NHS Concept and Its British Version

A National Health Service in its pure form is one in which the national government finances care, owns the facilities, and hires the providers on a salaried basis. The USSR (as we knew it) and Cuba are among the examples. It is a model not likely to receive much attention on Capitol Hill, both because of a "guilt by association" effect and because it is simply too wrenching a departure from America's pluralism.

In Great Britain, however, we find a variant that we can call "semisocialized" NHS, and although it is also politically quite beyond the pale for adoption here, it is well worth noting that approaches very different from our own can work well in other cultures.

Britain's NHS provides universal coverage (even for visitors from the United States), and there are only minor cost-sharing requirements. The basic revenue for the system comes from general national taxes. Britain's system clearly passes the fundamental test of medical effectiveness, as seen in comparative health status statistics. Britain's infant mortality rate in 1988, for example, was 9 deaths per

1,000 live births, comparing favorably with our 10 that year. Furthermore, this creditable rating consumed only about half the share of GDP taken by health care in the United States, and much less than half on a per capita basis: $836 there versus $2,354 here (1989).

How does NHS work in Britain? Government owns most of the hospitals, and their specialists are salaried. (Note that specialists—termed "consultants"—are normally hospital-based, and office-based primary physicians refer to them their patients needing hospitalization. This is the general European pattern, too.) The primary-care doctors are not, technically speaking, government employees but individual "contractors." They receive per capita payments for each patient signed up with them, and additional monies (about half their income) on an FFS basis for administering immunizations and performing preventive screening. Patients may freely choose their primary doctor; there are no HMO-like restrictions.

Because the government is a near-monopsonist (a single buyer of 90 percent of health care), it is in a position to use its budgeting process to implement medical priorities. Health care critics here can do little but wring their hands over the skewed use of money that supports high-tech procedures that briefly delay death for a few patients while ignoring primary-care needs of many others. But Britain can effectively prioritize universal primary care. For example, although Britain's system discourages duplicating expensive equipment like MRIs, it encourages development of geriatric services as the aging share of its population increases.

There is a private sector in British medicine. It includes both insurance that enables one to jump the "queue" (or waiting list) for major operations like hip replacement or cataract removal and a rather surprising private-public accommodation in which public hospitals set aside some "private pay" beds that specialists may use for their private patients. (This was one of the political compromises that smoothed the way for passage of the National Health Service legislation in 1948.)

Are there problems? From an American cultural perspective, yes. First and foremost is the queuing and technological rationing. In the United States, someone (a well-insured someone, that is) told today that she needs open heart surgery or a knee replacement expects to begin treatment within a few days. To wait months or more than a year would be unthinkable. Or if diagnosis might be even marginally more certain by use of an MRI-scan, the American patient would not accept being told that there aren't enough machines and he will have to wait or go ahead without that further testing assurance.

Britain can abide these kinds of limitations (which are also a major means by which it avoids our expenditure rate) because both physicians and patients are less aggressive than we in health care approach, and their tradition of deference to authority is matched by our opposite tradition of challenging anyone—especially anyone representing government—who tells us we cannot do what we want, have what we want. It is not accident but a deep cultural difference that has made workable for them a pattern that would be rejected here. (However, circumstances may be leading both extremes toward a middle ground over the next few years.)

At another level, their centralization combined with a less aggressive posture produces a considerably less innovative research and technology thrust. In their tighter system of political controls there is simply less "wiggle room" for the kind of freewheeling congressional politics that has produced the immense National Institutes of Health budget for biomedical research. And there is less administrative leeway for the organizational experiments that have produced HMOs, PPOs, and Community Health Centers.

So semisocialized medicine in Great Britain has much to recommend it, but it probably is not for us. In line with the adage "no pain no gain," the gains come at too much pain for those accustomed to the U.S. way of doing things.

NHI: The Canadian Case

The most attractive features of the Canadian National Health Insurance system from a patient viewpoint are that it covers all citizens and legal residents and has very little cost-sharing by patients. Just present your card to the doctor or hospital of your choice and receive the care you need. That's it.

No matter where you live, the program covers almost all normal doctor and hospital services. The most significant exclusions are prescription medications and dental services. Canadian Medicare (the name they use for their program, not to be confused with our Medicare program for the elderly) also has some advantages from a doctor's viewpoint. It is a fee-for-service system in which doctors remain independent professionals. Because everyone is covered, the physician is sure to be paid; and she does not face a bewildering array of insurance company forms to fill out with varying criteria imposed by payers looking over her shoulder. Canada has sufficient overall budget controls so that the national government has not been as intrusive at the doctor-patient level as are American insurers seeking cost containment.

Like the United States and unlike Britain, Canada is a federation. Its 10 provinces are like our 50 states, and they supply more than half the health care system's funding. There is therefore more regional variation than Americans longing for a single national system seem to have realized. Physicians' fees, for example, are negotiated at the provincial level.

In this context, private insurance exists only at the fringes, somewhat like Medigap policies here. In almost all corporations employee benefits include one or more of the following: dental services, prescription drugs, and semiprivate accommodations.

Among some U.S. advocates of the Canadian system, there is an apparent assumption that what exists as a full-blown system there might be imported in one fell swoop. That's unlikely, to say the least; and it may be a good reality check for us to note that our northern neighbor's system took several decades to get where it is today, starting from Saskatchewan's municipal doctor plan in 1914. The first hospital plan was adopted in that same province in 1947, and national hospital coverage was adopted in 1957, becoming a reality in all provinces by 1961. Not until 10 years later were physician services added.

Although U.S. Medicare is actually NHI for the elderly and disabled, universalizing it and making it compulsory and exclusive in its coverage would be not just an incremental but a radical change. First, universal Medicare would be even more nationalized than Canada's plan, which is operated by the provinces, not the national government. And it would require much higher taxes and would greatly disrupt the private insurance industry. However, the differences that would most dampen enthusiasm for the Canadian system lie in political and economic values.

Equality and the good of the whole nation define the Canadian people's social expectations. In health care, everyone belongs to the same plan and there is no means test (i.e., proof of very low income is not required for eligibility as with Medicaid in the United States). There are no hospitals with a primarily poor clientele. Indeed, Canada's egalitarian ethic goes further than Britain's: No private insur-

ance is permitted for services covered by the national plan; there are
no private-pay beds; and physicians who have NHI patients may not
also have private patients. An official 1983 statement expresses the
underlying social ethic: "The Government of Canada believes that a
civilized and wealthy nation . . . should not make the sick bear the
financial burden of health care. Everyone benefits from the security
and peace of mind that comes with having prepaid insurance. The
misfortune of illness, which at some time touches each of us, is
burden enough: the cost of care should be borne by society as a
whole."

The American expectation, however, is defined by individualism,
political and economic, with the result that for all the vocalized
concern about the uninsured, we have not been willing to give
coverage for everyone a priority over economic privatism, and we
continue to accept all the anomalies of expensive high-tech procedures for some while others go without primary care. Canada ensures availability of primary care but offers much slower access to
high-tech medicine because of its limited economic resources. The
waiting lists that result are indignantly pointed to by some U.S.
observers as an unacceptable aspect of NHI. The Canadian response
is articulated well by Dr. Morton Lowe, coordinator of health sciences at the University of British Columbia: "You have to wait your
turn [in Canada] for a hip transplant even if there are three poorer
people in front of you. Which I think is damn fine. In the U.S., if
you're rich, you get it fast, and if you're poor, you don't get it at all.
That's how they ration."[2]

Another basic political value that creates much hesitancy about
adopting the Canadian system, even among many who acknowledge
its very real virtues, is our basic distrust of government. This goes
beyond popular ideology: Political scientists perceive American administrative capacity as less than that of many other nations, in
good part because of what is called the permeability of administration by pluralistic group pressures, which impede rational implementation even of good legislation. Canadians, having both a social
democratic party on the left and a paternalistic kind of conservatism
on the right, see government in a positive light and assume it can do
an effective job. Thus the enabling legislation for Canada's system
required that each province's program be publicly administered.
Robert G. Evans, a leading health economist who is a Canadian, puts
it this way: "As residents of a small country heavily dependent on

world markets, flanked on the north by a large and hostile wilderness and on the south by a large—and, well, large—neighbor, Canadians have instinctively turned to the state as the instrument of collective purposes."[3] "Instinctively turn to the state"—? A phrase most unlikely to be used in the United States, and a strong symbolic expression of the chasm to be crossed before the Canadian model in its full form could be adopted here.

NHI: A Physician-sponsored Plan

The most widely publicized effort to design a U.S. version of the Canadian system is that of Physicians for a National Health Program (PNHP).[4] The major features of its National Health Program (NHP) would be universal coverage and a broad scope of services (the usual hospital and physician services plus prescriptions, preventive measures, and long-term care); exclusivity (private insurance eliminated for services included in NHP); no deductibles or copayments; free choice of provider by patients; and free choice of work pattern (e.g., fee-for-service, salaried in an HMO or a clinic) for physicians.

This very extensive package would be publicly financed from national, state, and even local government taxes, all going into a single national fund with an annually determined cap to enforce budgetary discipline. Each state would have a single public insurer to which the central office in Washington would allocate funds under a formula taking into account age patterns, income level, and other factors for each state's population. Hospitals and physician representatives would negotiate annual budgets and fee schedules with the state insurer. Giving a substantial role to the states accords well with our decentralization preference and is a political mark in this proposal's favor as compared with more thoroughly national plans.

Anticipated billing simplification and administrative cost savings are at the heart of this proposal's projected financing of extensive benefits. The appealing claim regarding billing is expressed in this manner: "Itemized patient-specific hospital bills would become an extinct species. . . . The effort and expense of [FFS physician] billing would be trivial: stamp the patient's NHP card on a billing form, check a diagnosis and a procedure code, send in all bills once a week, and receive full payment for virtually all services—with an extra payment for any bill not paid within 30 days."

Regarding administrative costs, this proposal projects savings in the total health care system of $40 billion from the efficiencies of single-payer budgeting and negotiated budgets, plus perhaps $27 billion from the elimination of private insurance overhead and profits. Figuring that $12 billion would be needed to cover the previously uninsured, PNHP would then apply net savings of $55 billion to provide program expansions (e.g., LTC, prescription drugs) within the existing total national health expenditure.

A great-sounding plan—on the benefits side. But perhaps not so great from a financial-political perspective. Although the proposing group addresses some of the likely objections to its proposal, its responses seem to include some wishful thinking and to avoid some issues.

To begin with, the administrative savings estimate is overly optimistic. There is no doubt whatsoever that a single-payer system, and one that did not have to include marketing costs, competitive duplication of facilities and equipment, and a profit expectation, would trim costs substantially. However, the historical power of American interest groups generally and of the AMA in particular does not support the assumption, for example, that if simplified billing reduced physician expenses by 6.25 percent, then physicians' bargaining representatives would accept a reduction in their gross incomes by that amount. It is far more likely that the physicians' representatives would successfully insist on splitting the difference, and so would the hospitals.

Furthermore, Canada's low administrative costs are obtained partly by not gathering all the utilization review statistics that we do. We would surely continue this process as an essential ingredient of analyzing the effectiveness of competing treatment modes. Also, we have far more constituency intervention in administration by local, state, and national politicians, which means that criteria other than efficiency would prevent costs from reaching any theoretical low point. Contingency fee lawsuits—not allowed in Canada—would also muddy the administrative waters by requiring some continuation of defensive practices.

The larger feasibility problems concern the politics of taxation. PNHP proposes to continue using federal individual and corporate income taxes, state sales taxes, local property taxes, and gasoline-alcohol-tobacco levies to pay for health expenditures in their existing proportions. The amounts represented by the Medicare portion of Social Security payroll taxes (about $72 billion in 1991) and employer-employee private insurance premiums (about $187 billion) would also be retained, but the combination of these would be rolled into a single payroll tax paid jointly by employers and employees. Finally, to produce about one-fifth of the needed monies, PNHP puts forward a smorgasbord of seven new taxes (in lieu of existing out-of-pocket expenses) that would include a 38 percent federal income tax bracket; a limit on mortgage interest deductions; a transfer tax on securities; energy taxes; increased excise taxes on alcohol and cigarettes; a new excise tax on pollutants; and a tax on fossil fuels.

The state of the federal budget constitutes a compelling obstacle in itself to establishing new taxes totaling over $300 billion for health care alone. To this, add the antitax mentality rampant at all levels and the competition for funding from the sectors of infrastructure repair, housing, and transportation.

It does not help to argue that the proposed taxes would be a shift in form of payment from private to public rather than a net additional cost to the public. Ideology makes such a shift anything but simple. People would perceive a new lack of individual control over how they spend their money, and the new taxes would be much more visible and resented than the money we currently spend out-of-pocket.

Leaving the aggregate of health care expenditures alone in a shift from private to public expenditure would mask tremendous shifts in who bears the burden. Those working in firms that have borne the entire expense of employee-benefit coverage would be paying a new payroll tax; those who have had deductibles and copayments would gain from the proscription of cost-sharing. Firms that are self-insured or that have developed cost-effective plans that may cost them less than their share of the new payroll tax would object vehemently to becoming part of the health care commons. Along the same lines, labor unions that have bargained fiercely over a period of years to obtain good health benefits would resist a de facto pay cut if cash compensation stayed the same but the government took over health expenses from the employer. Or else employers would resist having to pay more in after-tax cash wages to equal their workers' loss of pretax "income" in the form of health benefits.

Politically, the PNHP proposal compounds the inevitable difficulties of its tax burden with the complexity and sheer number of tax changes to be made. Given our dismal failure to raise gasoline taxes

enough to reduce the increasingly high level of oil importation even
when that failure became a major factor leading us into the Gulf
War, how can one expect to impose new taxes on fossil fuels and to
increase energy taxes generally? And when we can't agree on even
one new federal tax, to propose seven new ones is to assume a
near-revolution in public and legislative attitudes.

I assume that PNHP would be flexible as to details and could
perhaps come up with financing patterns more feasible than those
in the present version of the plan.[5] But no matter how the details
might change, the proposal is so ambitious in public financing and
on the benefits side that it is much more likely to play the role of an
ultimate scenario than of a live legislative vehicle in the current
financial-political situation. (Senator Bob Kerry [D., Neb.] has en-
dorsed a plan called "Health USA"[6] that would also be entirely
publicly financed but would emphasize use of competing prepaid
group plans, as in the Enthoven plan discussed further on.)

UHI: The German Version

Only recently receiving attention among U.S. policymakers is Germany's intriguing approach (developed in the former West Germany). With financing that is technically private, though governmentally authorized, and operations parameters set by the central
government, the German system of "sickness funds" illustrates well
the Universal Health Insurance (UHI) model. Surprisingly, it may
present a more instructive parallel in some ways for the United
States than does Canada's scheme.

Like our system, it is very decentralized. Over 1,100 nonprofit
sickness funds constitute the insuring bodies, and they negotiate fees
with 19 regional organizations of ambulatory physicians. Germany's
system is also privately operated. The sickness funds and physician
associations are private, not governmental. Finally, their system is
also employment-related (for the most part).

Unlike in either the United States or Canada, German law mandates
a compulsory system, then delegates its operation to the nongovernmental sickness funds and regional physician associations.

Membership in the system is compulsory for all working persons
and their dependents with incomes below about $37,000 and for all
employers, with whom employees split the insurance premium costs
(averaging 12.8 percent of total costs, combined) on a 50–50 basis.

About 8 percent of the population are exempt and use private insurance, and the funds cover about 88 percent; the remainder are civil servants under a separate plan. (Near-universal coverage did not spring up overnight in Germany, either. It had the earliest beginning [1883], but only for lower-income blue-collar workers, with transport and office workers added in 1903, dependents of fund members in 1930, and farmworkers and salespeople in 1972.)

Although Germany's system is employment-related and uses employers as premium (= tax) collectors, workers from a number of employers are generally grouped under local area funds (about 265 of them). Some 700 larger (over 450 workers) firms have their own funds, and many white-collar workers are covered by separate national funds, as are some craft workers. Because of such arrangements, it is more accurate to call Germany's system occupational- rather than employer-related. Unemployed and retired persons continue to be covered by sickness funds obtained from pension funds and government payments and collected from the working cohort. Changing jobs therefore does not threaten one's coverage.

Each sickness fund managing team calculates the money needed for the next fiscal year and is empowered by law to set a payroll deduction contribution rate to match the need. The team then negotiates a binding budget with the regional ambulatory physician association (through which the doctors self-regulate their fees within that budget cap) and per diem rates with hospitals.

This combination of "private taxation" and compulsory group negotiation of fees constitutes what political scientists term "corporatism"—a cooperative relationship between private economic groups and government in which each is dependent on, and has obligations to, the other. Extensive grants of authority to such bodies, and compulsory membership, create a group pluralism differing substantially from the much more individualistic pluralism with which we are familiar. In ours, each group is expected to be out for itself, and mutual obligations with government are rarely a part of the bargain.

The funds' scope of coverage is comprehensive. It includes dental care, prescriptions, medical appliances, maternity and even funeral benefits, and preventive measures, as well as the expected acute hospital and ambulatory care. But remember: The employed patient-consumer contributes one-half the premium cost. There are also some minimal copayments—such as $7 per day (from $3.50

before 1989) for hospital visits—and these have been rising. (Preventing overutilization is seen as primarily the provider's professional responsibility.)

The attractiveness of the German system is that so much of it is privately operated yet it manages to provide near-universal coverage. The premium contributions are not—technically speaking—taxes, and the detailed running of the system is largely left to the funds, the associations, and the hospitals—private groups. The pluralism of insurers and of physician groups has some of the administrative cumbersomeness found in the operation of our 1,500 private insurance plans but presumably also some of the flexibility.

This dependence on nongovernmental intermediaries would be difficult, if not impossible, to copy here, however, for we lack the tradition of occupational and social solidarity that is strongly exemplified in Germany. Every physician must belong to a regional association there; here, only half of all physicians belong to the AMA, and specialty groups often challenge its claim to represent all doctors. Although private insurance companies negotiate fees with individual providers here, we would likely not be able to make insurer negotiation with state medical and hospital associations legally binding without direct government regulation. Paradoxically, although we like to see most activity in the private sector, when we view something as the public's business, we rarely want to use private authority to accomplish it.

Also, the 50–50 contribution system—to which all must belong and in which employee contributions are not related to number of family members and therefore are redistributive in favor of larger families—emphasizes the obligation of each member of society to share in the common burden. This ethic is, again, not as notable in the United States as are efforts by insurers to cream-skim and by payers to avoid cross-subsidization.

However, some of what Germany does by negotiation we may be able to do through public regulation—fee schedules and volume standards for physicians, for example. We can't—and would not want to—copy the German pattern in detail. We can and should learn what we can from it as a system that combines pluralism, major private-sector roles, and coverage for everyone at a cost that is both lower and more stable than ours.

UHI: The Play-or-Pay Approach

Let's turn now to some UHI-type proposals currently receiving attention in this country. Such plans mix public and private financing and operation.

It was not long ago that mandating health care coverage (meaning that employers must offer health insurance as an employee benefit) attracted renewed attention (after languishing since first proposed two decades ago) because of the knowledge that three-fourths of the uninsured are employed. Yet mandating has already been displaced as the "reform of choice" in current discussions by what are called "play-or-pay" plans. Why? Because of the growing realization that mandating as such does nothing for the remaining one-fourth of the uninsured who are not employed.

Play-or-pay (PoP) proposals require that employers either buy health insurance for their employees or pay a tax that will be used to fund a publicly administered alternative program. The resulting mix would not be a uniform national system, but it would provide universal coverage if the public segment was designed as a residual category including everyone not in an employer plan.

Politically, play-or-pay has the advantage of building on the private employment base and the disadvantage of having to raise the tax issue. The extent of added political difficulty deriving from antigovernment sentiments would vary with the particular provisions of each plan, such as whether the public segment was nationally or state-run.

Employer reactions would obviously depend partly on whether a firm was already providing insurance benefits and on its present margin of profitability. However, if there is to be any mandate at all, play-or-pay may be preferred because the choice of buying insurance or paying a known and presumably stable rate of taxation would provide something highly desirable to employers: a way to avoid the annual escalation of private insurance premiums. Because there would be some expansion in business purchases of private insurance, and the public-sector alternative might draw upon private insurers as administrative agents, insurance industry objections might be at least partially mitigated.

From an employee perspective, those currently not able to obtain group coverage through their employers would be the obvious gainers (along with their nonemployed dependents); some of the employed uninsured would doubtless object to paying a share (perhaps

20–25 percent) of premiums or additional taxes (required in many proposals), as would employees now in plans fully paid by the employer.

Let's look at three illustrative PoP schemes.

The Rockefeller-Pepper Commission Plan

We start with the widely publicized 1990 Pepper Commission Report (officially, the U.S. Bipartisan Commission on Comprehensive Health Care), whose majority recommendations have been presented in summary form by the commission's chairman, Senator John D. Rockefeller IV (D., W. Va.).[7]

Perceiving Medicaid expansion as a minimalist approach that would be least disruptive but quite inadequate, and NHI as desirable for its universalism but too controversial to be politically feasible, the Pepper Commission majority positioned its recommendations for play-or-pay as a medical and political middle ground. The commission would mandate employer coverage in firms of 100 or more employees after only a brief "adjustment" (i.e., get used to the idea) period. For smaller businesses, the mandate is a "soft" one encouraging voluntary action through private insurance reforms, tax breaks, and subsidization of premiums for firms with fewer than 25 workers. After four or five years, the mandate would become "hard" if less than 80 percent of workers (and dependents) in the smaller firms had not become insured. So that employers would not then be at the mercy of ever-escalating private insurance providers, the Pepper Commission's pay alternative would allow them to opt for buying public coverage in a new federal program, for which they would pay a specified percentage of payroll. Set at a level to encourage continuation of private coverage, the payroll tax would cap the employer obligation and pressure private insurers to keep their costs competitive.

The federal program would replace Medicaid and serve the non-employed, the self-employed, and workers whose employers could not afford private insurance premiums. Because it would include workers and private employer financing, the new public program would no longer be "just a welfare program." States would possibly object to this new federal program because they would lose the authority they now have over Medicaid. These concerns would be assuaged by limiting state financial contributions to their present levels. Both private and public insurance would have to cover federally defined minimum benefits, including preventive services such as Pap smears, mammograms, and children's immunizations. (The idea of prevention is catching on: Many of the reform proposals include it.) Patients would not be without cost-sharing responsibilities, which could include 20 percent of the premiums, plus deductibles and coinsurance, but the near-poor would pay on a sliding scale and there would be no copayments for those in poverty.

On the con side, the Rockefeller-Pepper Commission proposal shares with the AMA's mandate plan a failure to specify a federal funding source for its approximate price tag of $24 billion and to set forth strong measures to contain costs. It would thus be no more likely to achieve passage in its original form.

A similar plan advanced by Senate majority leader George J. Mitchell (D., Me.) with support from Senators Kennedy and Rockefeller was approved in January 1992 by a Senate committee on a party-line vote as an opening salvo from the Democrats in the election-year health care battle. Also play-or-pay, it would establish a new "Americare" public program, to be operated by the states, for everyone under 65 not covered by employment-based insurance. It tries to do more about cost control by proposing a National Health Care Expenditure Board to set spending goals through provider-government negotiations at the state level. But this is largely smoke and mirrors, as they say in Washington, because the goals are only that; they are not controls.

Enthoven's Managed Competition Framework

A very different play-or-pay approach is the "managed competition" concept strongly advocated, with much public attention both here and abroad, by Alain C. Enthoven, a business economist at Stanford University.[8] His mixture of governmental and market competitive elements seems to be focused overwhelmingly on cost control, with broadened patient access a secondary objective.

Enthoven's "consumer choice" scheme begins with mandated private coverage of full-time employees (with the employer's premium pegged at 80 percent of the cost of an average group health plan and employees paying the rest of the cost of whichever plan they choose), plus an 8 percent payroll tax on wages of part-time and seasonal employees if they are not included. With these tax

revenues, plus 8 percent of income contributed by the self-employed, early retirees, and other nonemployed persons (with sliding-scale subsidies for the poor and near-poor), the federal government would make payments to the states. Each state would establish
a public sponsor, that is, an agency that would contract with private-sector managed-care plans to enroll former Medicaid patients,
the self-employed, and workers whose small-business employers
found that they could get a better buy from the public sponsor than
from the private insurance marketplace. Everyone could then be
covered, privately or publicly, and the costs would be kept down,
according to the logic of the plan, by price competition among
HMOs competing for contracts with the states and large private
employers.

The major strength of Enthoven's plan is that, like other
play-or-pay schemes, it builds on the employment base. If its organizational competition would work as he anticipates, then it would do
what we want: cover everyone and control costs.

The weaknesses are that the competition is unlikely to work, yet
the effort would radically (more radically than a Canadian-style
public system) transform the context in which most health professionals operate while denying to most Americans freedom of provider choice.

Surely the desire to retain that choice is a major reason HMOs
have not shown consistent national growth. They seem to have
strongholds in a few places—California, the Twin Cities area of
Minnesota, and the Seattle area stand out—because of local history
and culture. Encouraged by the Reagan administration, a new set of
profit-oriented HMOs (the best known, and arguably the best, earlier
ones were nonprofit) arose in the mid-1980s. But these HMOs were
without notable cost savings, sometimes generated considerable
scandal because of their marketing practices, and experienced a
much-slowed rate of growth as the 1990s began.

The lack of HMOs in much of the country makes one wonder just
how realistic Enthoven's plan is. Where there are not multiple HMOs
to compete, how is the plan to work? Where HMOs do exist, will
they compete to get clients in rural or inner city areas? small
business clients? clients with above-average numbers of older workers? And would not price competition give each HMO an incentive
to offer only very minimal benefit packages in order to keep its price
down?

"Managed competition" is, after all, a paradoxical concept. Conceptually, a competitive economy stands in strong contrast to a managed economy. Enthoven wants to manage the competition, however, because he acknowledges that health care insurance competition is, left to its own devices, neither efficient nor fair. It "cannot work at the individual level," he has written. That is why he turns to the oxymoronic concept of managed competition, with the managing done by large corporations and public sponsors. They are to be charged with the responsibility of being "intelligent, active, collective purchasing agents" on our behalf. This compels private businesses to make sophisticated judgments, medical and financial, on details of health care. Although a few very large employers are hiring health care professionals to design their insurance programs, it is most unlikely that very many firms will be able or willing to become health managers on such a scale *on behalf of their workers* as distinct from just being money managers for themselves.

Apart from the economics, shouldn't we worry about the possible impact on the human and humane qualities of health care if we so strongly place all physicians and other providers in a context that creates pressures to sacrifice professionalism on the altar of price competition and a bottom-line business ethic? Does it really make sense to rest our hopes on what may be just an economist's wistful thinking on the cost-control side and highly disruptive to patients and professionals on the care side?

"An American Approach"

A third major play-or-pay plan is offered by John Holahan and his associates[9] in a long-standing health policy group at The Urban Institute (a politically middle-of-the-road think tank) in Washington, D.C. What they have named "An American Approach" combines public and private incentives in a sophisticated (if rather complex) way and offers a cost-control system borrowing from Canadian experience.

Employers (perhaps even those with just one employee) would be required to pay 75 percent of insurance meeting federally defined benefit standards, and employees would be obligated to purchase it with a copremium not exceeding 25 percent of the cost (with subsidies for low-income workers). Or the employer could pay a state tax of about 7 percent of payroll that would (with required employee contributions on a sliding scale) be used to fund a variety of new state-selected public plans. Replacing Medicaid, the state plans would enroll workers whose employers chose to pay the tax, along with former Medicaid patients and other nonworkers choosing to buy into the plans on a sliding scale. Everyone would be required to belong to an employer-provided group or the public plan, and all would contribute within their means. (Medicare would stay in place for the elderly.)

The payroll tax rate should, in Holahan's view, be low enough to encourage a substantial minority of employers to prefer it to private insurance. (Note the contrast with the Rockefeller-Pepper plan on this point.) Holahan estimates that as much as one-third of the nonelderly might be included in the public plans, creating substantial political support because participating patients would include many taxpayers.

The benefits would include the usual acute services, excluding prescription drugs (at least initially) but adding prevention measures. There would be a deductible and a 20 percent copayment up to a stop-loss limit varying with income and size of family. Firms could offer fuller programs, but the actuarial value of the enrichments would count as taxable income. (And this might lead to some reduction in scope of coverage for those who had previously enjoyed the most generous plans.) Long-term care, now a major state expense of Medicaid programs, would become a national government responsibility. This change would release about the amount of money needed to cover the added acute care costs of the new state programs.

The federal government would award grants to states equaling 60 percent of the total public program costs, with more subsidy to poor states and less to the better-off ones. The funds would come from an earmarked national sales or payroll tax.

The major element borrowed from Canada is federal grants not as open-ended entitlements, as with Medicaid, but as annual adjustments in order not to exceed the national GNP growth rate. Having to absorb all costs beyond national GNP growth, the states would have a strong incentive to explore a variety of cost-effectiveness possibilities. A further ripple effect is that insurance companies would have an incentive to work with providers on cost control and to keep their own premiums competitive in order to avoid losing market share to the public plan. Each state would be free to pursue its own route to cost containment by trying a regulatory approach or contracting with private HMOs or PPOs as a way of testing managed competition on a limited scale.

All in all, this is an ambitious proposal and one worked out in considerable detail. Its complexity is probably both its strength and its weakness.

This plan combines mandating, obligatory universal enrollment in one or another plan, retention of Medicare as a known quantity for the elderly, a federalized LTC, a nationally defined scope of benefits that covers not just the poor, and a cap on federal spending. The plan would preserve the private insurance industry and permit diversity among the states in how they handle their program responsibilities. All-or-nothing debates about program design and cost-control methods among contending interests at the national level might thus be defused. These are all major advantages, programmatically and politically, but they are only made possible through complicated intermingling of various elements.

On the con side, states would have to raise more revenue and would surely object to being placed at risk for cost increases beyond GNP growth. The new federal tax, along with required employee contributions, would bring pained outcries, even though out-of-pocket expenditures would be much less for many people (though greater for some). The net additional costs of the proposal would be something over $25 billion; a large amount, but not in the same league as public financing needed for a Canadian-style NHI. Major changes in the operations of employers, state governments, and insurance companies, and in the federal-state mix of responsibilities, plus the sheer number of different enactments required at all levels to get the program into being, would be very large hurdles. The total package is well balanced, but delicately so; failure to succeed in passing any one part might well threaten the effectiveness of the entire system. In short, an intriguing but risky gamble.

The Mandate Approach

Mandating that employers provide health insurance for employees (who may also be required to contribute) was for years the primary alternative advocated by those who recognized the problem of the uninsured but rejected publicly funded NHI approaches. In a way, it seems the obvious way to go when one recalls that three-fourths of the uninsured are either employed or dependents of employed persons.

In 1971, an employer mandate was urged on Congress with the rationale that it would simply be "one step further" along the path of social protections long since taken by mandated minimum wages, child labor laws, disability and Social Security retirement contributions, and occupational safety and health standards. Who was the proposer? President Richard M. Nixon, who saw mandating as a way of keeping health care in the private sector while broadening the population covered—and as a political response to the threat of NHI as represented in the Health Security Act then being pushed by Senator Edward M. Kennedy (D., Mass.).

In the budgetarily strapped and ideologically more conservative environment of the late 1980s, however, Kennedy's advocacy shifted to a Basic Health Benefits Act that mandated employer coverage after many conservatives had moved away from requiring employer action.

Mandating's lead characteristic and strongest advantage is that it does not create any new public program or impose new taxes. The employer's contact with government is limited to providing evidence that insurance coverage (probably with legislatively specified minimum benefits and maximum employee cost-sharing limits) is being purchased for all employees working over a specified number of hours weekly. A parallel obligation could be imposed on workers to buy the insurance offered. No money is sent to the government; the coverage continues to be with the carrier of the employer's choice or by corporate self-insurance.

Although some conservatives would see mandating as a radical step, the more significant objection politically is not ideological but practical: the fear of small businesses that the higher costs they have to incur (because of experience rating and small size of groups) may undermine their profitability, or even their existence. Very large firms, however, are much more amenable to mandated coverage because they already provide it in most cases and see themselves as paying higher premiums because providers shift onto their policies the costs of serving the uninsured, who may well be the workers of smaller competitors.

Concern has also been expressed that some jobs would be lost because health care would tip total employment costs beyond the employer's acceptable limit for some low-wage work. Job turnover problems create another objection. Perhaps 20 million people are between jobs or self-employed at any one time, not to mention the fluctuation of unemployment involving more than a million workers for every unemployment percentage point up or down. The administrative complexity of tracking coverage could be a nightmare if seasonal and part-time workers were included in a mandated program. If they were excluded, only two-thirds of the uninsured would be reached through mandating.

Mandating: An AMA Plan

A specific example of the mandating approach is provided by the American Medical Association's Health Access America (HAA) proposal,[10] which attempts to improve access with minimal expansion of governmental roles. HAA would require coverage for full-time employees and their families by larger firms, then phase in small-business coverage with tax subsidies. Enrollees would share costs, with annual limits. There would be a standard benefit package for acute care, including prenatal, well-baby, and diagnostic services. The COBRA continuation law that enables former employees or their dependents to retain the employer's group rate would be amended to provide that the employer pay the premiums for the first four months after employment ends. However, AMA has called for limiting the employees' tax exemption on employer-provided health insurance to reduce "the tendency to overinsure [!] which occurs when an excessive number of ordinary, routine and highly predictable health services are covered by insurance."[11]

Medicaid would expand to cover all of the nonemployed poor, with a uniform set of benefits and a single-income eligibility standard. This change in Medicaid is proposed as the public-sector component in a number of plans, especially those from organizations that fear a more fundamental restructuring. For instance, in the summer of 1991 the heads of the AMA, AHA, HIAA, and BCBSA sent a joint statement to then–White House Chief of Staff John Sununu advocating such an expansion. Provider reimbursement in the reformed Medicaid would be at the generally higher Medicare rates. For the medically uninsurable and those ineligible for group coverage but unable to afford individual policies, state risk pools are urged, with subsidized premium assistance for those in the income range of 100–150 percent of poverty. Medicare would be improved by adding catastrophic benefits paid for by employer-employee contributions and by tax incentives to aid individuals in purchasing private nursing-home coverage.

On the financial side, the AMA expects new federal, state, and employer costs, but beyond estimating the federal share at perhaps $21 billion in 1990 dollars it forswears estimating total costs or suggesting revenue sources until the precise pattern of reforms has been determined.

The AMA clearly sees little need for substantial change. The political feasibility of its proposal is very slight, in good part because revenue sources for additional costs and cost-control propositions play so small a part as compared with expansion of benefits and increased provider payments under Medicaid. HAA's significance is less as a realistic vehicle for legislated reform than as a statement of one major interest group's suggestions of how to ensure a broader base of patients able to pay their bills.

Making Private Insurance More Accessible

After the Harris Wofford Senate victory in November 1991, Senator John H. Chafee (R., R.I.) led a group of Republican colleagues in proposing an ameliorating approach that would use new tax credits and deductions to aid families and small businesses in buying health insurance, regulate private insurance premiums, and double federal spending on community health centers and the National Health Service Corps—spending badly needed to serve poor neighborhoods and rural areas for which resources were sharply cut in the Reagan years. President Bush's 1992 proposals follow Chafee's lead. His sketchily developed plans would use tax credits of up to $3,700 per family as a vehicle for expanding the number of people covered by private insurance. Several million persons would still be without coverage, although this would enable some who cannot obtain coverage through employment to buy individual policies. There is no provision for an inflation adjustment and not even an assurance that the amounts offered would buy a good policy in all areas. To pay for the tax credits, President Bush states expectations of great savings from changes in state insurance laws, greater medical efficiency, and reductions in costs of Medicare and Medicaid. There is a total absence of any strong provision for cost controls within the private insurance market that the credits would subsidize. The administration's proposals constitute a political placeholder—a way of saying we are in this game—rather than a real legislative agenda.

Rising legislative and public concern about the shortcomings of private insurance marketing strategies, recognized in the administration's sudden interest in the topic, has become so strong that even private insurer trade associations are now trying to become part of the solution. Trade associations are partly motivated by the desire to ward off the long-range threat of a totally public NHI or play-or-pay UHI; more immediately, they want to avoid having potentially strong federal regulation supplant more industry-friendly state regulation that the insurance industry has enjoyed for half a century.

Representative of private insurance reform proposals is one presented on behalf of the Health Insurance Association of America (HIAA) by its executive director, Carl J. Schramm.[12] HIAA has 300 commercial insurer member firms and is the peak association of the industry. The primary thrust of its reforms is to make health insurance more affordable to small businesses and more open to all their workers, either voluntarily or through state requirements. More specifically, HIAA's package includes end exclusion of higher-risk individuals; no new restrictions when changing jobs or carriers; limits on experience rating so that small-group rates would not be impossibly higher than those for larger groups; and private reinsurance for high-risk groups and state high-risk pools for otherwise medically uninsurable persons. Another key feature that a number of insurers are pushing is severe cutbacks in state requirements regarding the range of services that must be offered in an insurance plan so that a "bare-bones" plan can be sold to very small businesses. HIAA is also lobbying in 15 states, from Alaska and California to New York and New Jersey, for legislation requiring that insurers offer coverage to businesses with as few as three employees.

The Blue Cross and Blue Shield Association (BCBSA) has developed similar proposals yet seems to be having an internal tug-of-war. At the same time as it is moving to reduce small-business premiums and increase open enrollment opportunities, the "Blues" have moved away from community rating (only 22 plans now use it out of 73) because they have lost market share (1984, 33 percent; 1990, 28 percent) to the commercial insurers who use experience rating. However, if the commercial firms truly do engage in some reform of exclusionary devices, BCBSA will be able to do more, too, while remaining competitive.

The insurance reform approach may be a good finger in the dike while larger reforms are awaited. And there is a better chance of early action on this part of the access problem than on any of the broader changes. Several political advantages make legislation attractive: Most of the reforms would cost government nothing; they would help small businesses, a constituency that every elected official strives to please; and the industry itself has acknowledged a need for change.

Whether the action will come from the states or from Congress is perhaps the primary remaining issue as I write. Some states are already moving: Vermont and Oregon have actually gone further than HIAA anticipated: They have legislated community rating. In Congress, two men with real clout, Senator Lloyd Bentsen (D., Tex.) and Representative Dan Rostenkowski (D., Ill.) have introduced bills requiring that insurers permit open enrollment, outlawing small-group rates more than 25 percent above community averages, and permitting self-employed persons to deduct 100 percent of their insurance premiums (a measure long overdue). HIAA hopes the states will act swiftly to forestall such national action.

However, that is unlikely, for earlier efforts at state-by-state re-forms in health care have demonstrated that about half would never act on their own. As I wrote this, the situation seemed to be that although 23 states had acted to permit the bare-bones plans to be sold, the industry was making very little headway in persuading businesses to adopt them. A *New York Times* article of November 10, 1991, reported that in Washington State only 2,300 employees had been signed up in the lower-cost plan, and half of those enrollments resulted from employers downgrading the coverage they provided from better plans, rather than increasing net additions to persons covered!

The Privatized, Individualized Approach

Finally, at the individualized end of the reform spectrum is a plan from the Heritage Foundation (a conservative think tank) that would replace employer-provided coverage with insurance purchased by individuals shopping around for the best buy to fit their family circumstances. As presented by Stuart M. Butler,[13] the plan elimi-nates tax exemption for employee benefit coverage but includes (complicated) tax credits in the personal income tax code, their size correlated with the share of income a family spends on health needs, and refunded if the credit exceeds the family's tax liability. In a curious amalgam of compulsion and libertarian individualism, the Heritage Foundation would require that heads of household enroll all family members in a federally prescribed basic benefits plan, with lowest-income families enrolled through the refundable tax credits or Medicaid.

The claimed advantages are that everyone could be covered regardless of whether they are employed; employed persons would avoid losing job coverage when changing or losing jobs because their insurance would be independent of their employment; and administrative costs would be far less because the price system would work more efficiently than do administrative controls.

Unfortunately, the mechanisms Butler suggests to operate this market individualism scheme assume far more consumer knowledge about buying a policy than is likely to exist. Butler's response to this objection—that consumers could buy from a trusted organization that would put together a group such as a trade union, farm bureau federation, church, or an alumni group—raises more problems than it solves. That is, in the face of all the abuses that competition now creates in private insurance markets, his plan would multiply the number of organizations that would have to be monitored for adherence to the federally prescribed norms. And there is no apparent reason to believe that these alternative organizations would do any better than employers as purchaser surrogates for their members. Further, the Heritage Foundation plan would also require incredibly complex arrangements to adjust payroll withholding to fit each employee's estimated tax credit, even involving the Internal Revenue Service in postponed payments to providers when an individual faced a cash crunch.

This proposal is politically unrealistic and would be an ineffective nightmare if it were enacted. Its contribution is, ironically, to demonstrate that extreme individualism won't work.

This smorgasbord of proposals illustrates all too well the diversity of ways that the access crisis might be addressed. Not all of them contain meaningful cost controls, and some do not explain where the money for expanded access is to come from. One thing they all do make clear is that our eventual means for achieving universal health care coverage is overwhelmingly likely to mix private- and public-sector elements rather than to pursue either direction exclusively.

The next step—before recommending a specific set of reform elements in the final chapter—is to look closely at the equivalent range of cost-containment ideas currently in use or being advocated, both here and abroad. Chapter 6 covers a variety of microlevel approaches addressing separate pieces of the problem; Chapter 7 brings up some macro-, or across-the-board, strategies.

6
Cutting Costs: Piecemeal Approaches

Why should we worry about costs?—not a silly question by any means. A payer's costs are a provider's income, and health care providers (and supporting staff) constitute the third largest American industry in employment terms. Approximately 8.5 million persons work in health services, with a higher than average proportion of women and ethnic minorities. And health care costs are income to manufacturers selling goods used in the medical sector—22 percent of Eastman Kodak's sales are accounted for by medical sales, mostly of x-ray film. As the automobile industry shrinks and we wring our hands over lost job opportunities, should we not equally celebrate the projections of ever-increasing health care expenditures with ever-increasing job opportunities—especially when we see that in the 12 months ended July 1991 health care jobs increased 4.9 percent while overall private jobs declined 1.3 percent?

Uwe E. Reinhardt has been pointing out for a decade the paradoxical character of the cost "crisis": We celebrate contributions to larger GNP in other industries yet deplore them in the case of health care. In macroeconomics—the discipline that looks at the aggregates of the economy—such a viewpoint is nonsense. There is surely as much reason to welcome an increase in the proportion of national income spent on medicine and therapeutic treatments as there is to applaud an increase in the proportion spent on Nintendo games, vintage wines, and imported luxury cars. If one worries about "crowding out" savings and investment, surely it would be better to cut back on the latter categories in order to increase national savings—but no one suggests that.

So what's the problem?

There are in fact several real problems stemming from certain peculiarities of health care, especially the nature of its market, how it is paid for, and the uncertainties of its effectiveness. Additional trouble arises from a weak economy and a disastrous national budget deficit.

In industries subject to even a reasonably close approximation of textbook price competition, sellers (providers, in our case) need to pare their costs to gain and keep customers. Health care's market is not of that type. Indeed, competition that takes the form of each hospital thinking it has to duplicate any equipment held by a rival is more likely to *raise* total costs. Cost controls thus have to come from outside.

Purchases of Nintendo games are made by individuals and reflect their desires and use of personal funds. Health care "purchases" are made mostly by insurers and the payers behind them and predominantly reflect choices made by seller-providers. Patients' funds constitute a lesser share, especially of the hospital charges that make up the area of greatest expense. Although the "moral hazard" argument is overused as a defense when loading more of total costs onto patients, it is true that a public accustomed to first-dollar or 80 percent coverage from a largely employer-paid insurance program will not be a strong economizing force on its own. The employer and government payers on whom the system's costs are concentrated do have a sense of organizational and financial crisis, and the payer revolt currently in full swing is producing a crisis for the public.

Business was slow in realizing the immensity of the commitments it was making as it kept expanding employee health care benefits after World War II, partly as a way of avoiding "government intrusion." But as premiums increase and profits decline, employers are alerted to the monster they have created. Any firm not already sensitized by its benefits manager is now getting the message from its chief accountant's wailing about the FASB (Federal Accounting Standards Board) requirement that future costs be recognized in the balance sheet. General Electric, for example, reduced its 1991 earnings by $1.8 billion in order to comply, and General Motors estimates its committed costs as being in the $16–$24 billion range. It has been estimated that the total corporate obligation will exceed $400 billion.

The national government also faces a cost crisis because it bears the financial responsibility for the majority of the elderly's medical expenses and of Medicaid outlays. As these expenses rise much faster than federal revenues, and the deficit negates any possibility of substantially expanding the federal budget, a zero-sum game is created. Each additional dollar spent on health care means the loss of a dollar from some other program area—and some areas such as housing, nutritional assistance, and education may do more for good health in the long run than more spent on physicians. Because the cost of health care is rising more rapidly than the costs of these other programs, it becomes a more inviting target.

Less obviously, the government faces a cost crisis in health care because of its overaccommodation to health care providers when Medicare was established. Had the system of basing reimbursement on historical charges been replaced with DRGs and fee schedules from the beginning, we would not be in so much of a pickle today. Providers (whose ranks include contractual vendors, profit-seeking testing companies, and manufacturers of medical devices, as well as physicians) must be expected to act like other participants in our self-interest-oriented economy; they like to maximize income as much as do the rest of us. Without effective price competition to hold down prices, cost control has to come from payer resistance to provider demands. It took us some years to learn that.

With knowledgeable analysts estimating that 20–30 percent of all health care is probably at least ineffective and that some of it is harmful, the need for greater cost-effectiveness in how employer and taxpayer dollars (as well as our direct dollars as patients) are spent is a very solid reason for working on cost containment. If we could substantially reduce the uncertainties of what works best and what does not work at all, many billions could be saved—perhaps enough to expand coverage to all the presently uninsured without a net increase in total system costs.

So there are a number of reasons we hear so much about the cost crisis and a variety of ways of seeking cost reduction. (Note that when we say cost reduction in this context, we most often mean a reduction in the rate of increase. With a growing, aging population and ever-greater intensity of what can be done, reduction in overall expenditures is not in the cards.)

The task now is to describe and evaluate the many roads to cost containment, examining each type in terms of both its cost impact and its health care implications. We can divide these into two distinct, if overlapping, types: the economic model and the medical model. The former includes propositions about financial behavior that are applied to health care (copayments are a good example) in an effort to reduce utilization, with the medical consequences considered as a by-product—if at all. If we use the medical model, we start with the practice of medicine and see how changes can be made that result in at least as good care for patients and in lower costs as a positive by-product. The presumption is that many expenses can be avoided if we learn which tests and treatments are either ineffective or inappropriate in a given circumstance and thus reduce uncertainty of treatment. Let's look at major thrusts within each of these models and at ways of combining them, because they can sometimes work together.

In this chapter, we'll look at partial cost controls: those that affect one or another specific item but do not directly affect the system as a whole. Approaches with a large potential for producing system-wide savings will be covered in Chapter 7.

The Economic Model—and Its Dangers

Cost Shifting Is Cost Avoidance, Not Cost Control

A preliminary warning is called for: Some of the rhetoric of cost containment—especially as voiced by payer representatives—is very misleading. There is a big difference between cost containment *for the whole system* and cost *avoidance* by particular payers. In our system of multiple payers, a strong buyer may reduce costs for itself by shifting them to other payers, but that may do nothing to reduce overall health care costs. Much that passes for cost control is really passing the buck.

From a payer's perspective, the simplest and most quickly effective way to trim costs or at least lessen the upward spiral is to make the consumers (the prospective patients) pay a larger share. In Chapters 3 and 4 we saw that corporations are pushing to increase employee cost-sharing by creating or increasing deductibles and copayments, making first-dollar coverage a thing of the past except where collective bargaining is strong enough to insist on its retention. And some are even requiring full employee payment for dependents' premiums and abandoning the field of retiree coverage for new hires. The only way that such actions can reduce system costs is by reducing access. Some firms (especially small ones) may be able to rationalize the "dump it on the employees" approach as necessary for business survival, but that does not make increased patient cost-sharing an effective or legitimate way to control costs for the nation. Corporations are joined in this strategy by state and national governments, creating the inequities and inadequacies we have seen in Medicare and Medicaid programs.

One economic-model approach sometimes advocated both to reduce the national government's deficit and to discourage "overinsurance" removes or limits the tax subsidy for health insurance. About $38 billion per year in revenues is lost because of deductions for health insurance costs. Although it is true that this subsidy aids the wealthier employees the most, without it many employers might not offer health insurance at all, or the employee share would be much greater—which would be much more of a hardship on lower-wage workers. Anyway, this approach just does not comport with political reality.

True believers in economic incentives will assert that cost-sharing is not just cost-shifting but a necessary part of cost containment because it avoids excessive utilization and higher expenditures brought about through moral hazard. But as noted earlier, the individual patient's role in moral hazard is minimal; and making the patients pay more is a poor way to deter providers from overdoing their services. If out-of-pocket payments were nearly as effective in deterring possible overuse as advocates claim, there should be very little overuse in the United States. The 27 percent we already pay is far greater than the 5.8 percent in Britain, the 12 percent in Germany, or the 19 percent in Canada.

Even if, as some observers think, reduced use of health care because of patient sharing reflects unneeded and even harmful treatment as much as it does loss of necessary care, it is an improper and blunderbuss approach. So long as the efficacy of much medical treatment is uncertain, it is surely better that health care financing err, if at all, on the side of seeing that everyone needing treatment gets it than on the side of saving money for payers at the risk of leaving needy patients without health care.

One more reason for being skeptical about copayments is their inefficiency. One RAND study found that 70 percent of hospital costs were incurred by 10 percent of the patients, which means that many of the copayments could not have saved much (though they may have deterred a low-income patient from receiving treatment) and that the bulk of expenditures in high-cost cases would have been exempted by exceeding the stop-loss threshold.

A Legitimate Role for Cost-Sharing

Despite the self-serving nonsense of payers calling cost-dumping onto patients cost containment, there is a legitimate—I think even morally and politically necessary—role for cost-sharing if carried out in a way that does not prevent necessary utilization. That way is through the employee's premium contribution, which is paralleled by the Medicare portion of Social Security withholding. Advocates of national health insurance for the United States often neglect to note that the broader coverage provided in other nations is accompanied by substantial taxation and/or substantial premium-sharing—such as the 50 percent sharing of the German system. Beyond saving money for employers, a 20 percent employee share of premium costs (the figure most commonly suggested) would serve to sensitize employees to health care costs by reflecting each year the impact that a higher or lower rate of utilization has on the next year's premium cost. This might thereby lessen whatever real waste there may be from the consumer side of moral hazard (and thus indirectly also reduce employer costs). This form of cost-sharing is tied to an annually set payroll deduction and thus can effectively balance legitimate concerns about employee inattention to costs with the need to avoid deterring patients from seeking care because of out-of-pocket expenses at the point of receiving service.

Putting the patient's share of costs into the premium is also far superior to copayments at the time of treatment because costs are then predictable. What most of us want in health insurance is not simply coverage of a risk; it is the security of knowing that when ill health strikes it need not mean the disruption of the household budget, which is often enough in precarious shape anyway these days. Those who assert that individuals should be able to handle minor, "ordinary" medical expenses without insurance are foolishly ignoring this element. If we know how much the expense will be so that we can budget for it, yes, we can handle it. But anything unbudgetable is scary.

Another good reason for this kind of cost-sharing is that it engenders and supports a sense of self- and community responsibility, and of social solidarity. Assuming that premium-sharing would take place within insurance reforms requiring community rating in group policies so that we know we are all in this together, it could likely play a substantial role in legitimizing a mandated-coverage approach to UHI, as well as in contributing to cost control. Cost-sharing can be a good thing, as well as a mere cost-shifting ploy, if done in the right way.

Structuring a More Effective Market

As individuals, we don't know enough about either medicine or its providers to be cost-effective purchasers of our own health care by making providers compete for our "business." But in the "managed competition" espoused by Enthoven as a way of both insuring everyone and saving money, competition is supposed to control costs if employers or other sponsoring organizations do the "purchasing" of health care for us, that is, they select an HMO they then offer to individuals. The problems with this approach were touched on in Chapter 5. Another competition concept, less tied to HMOs, is what Walter McClure has dubbed the "prudent buyer" approach. Employers would act on our behalf in their role as contractors for group health coverage plans, setting up networks (essentially PPOs) of the *best* providers. The key lies in developing solid information about hospitals, doctors, and other providers—not just about their prices but about their quality and efficiency as seen in the outcomes of their work with patients. With such information, employers could reward with contracts those providers who deliver quality care, steering enough patients to them to gain their cooperation in discounting their fees.

To make this possible, coalitions of employers must pool their employees' treatment records to produce a statistically significant data base, and such efforts are under way in a number of locations. Along this line, Medicare has been releasing hospital mortality data in recent years, claiming that it may be helpful to patients, purchasers, and providers. The hospitals, asserting that the data do not adjust adequately for varying severity of illnesses among different patient groups, are less than enthusiastic about the program.

If employers and insurers are going to use PPOs and similar networks of providers who discount their fees as a major cost-containment thrust, it would clearly be helpful if they based their selections of providers on information about quality, instead of defining a "preferred" provider simply as one who meets formal credentials requirements and is willing to accept a reduced fee. But one has to doubt that enough user-friendly information will be available in enough locations to make this a major approach in the foreseeable future—any more than there are likely to be enough hospitals in any one location to provide a basis for competition. As of 1986, 40 percent of all community hospitals had no more than one competitor in a 15-mile radius, and small hospitals (fewer than 100 beds) got 70 percent of their admissions from only five physicians. (Perhaps too much of health care discussion is by analysts who live in densely populated cities and who forget that we still have many areas without the plethora of facilities that urbanites take for granted.)

Beyond all these factors, will employees have the knowledge required to be prudent buyers of the competing plans offered by an employer? Or are we then back to square one? And note that more knowledgeable patients tend to be more demanding patients: Insurers sometimes try to avoid health care professionals as subscribers for this reason!

Competition to provide the best quality is surely a good thing, and efforts should be made to use economic incentives to encourage it; but market competition as a general solution to cost problems has too many negatives to make it a good basic strategy. Non–price competition—as when all hospitals get the same per diem or the same DRG—produces a race to impress both physicians and patients with the newest and best technology and to spend money on marketing that might better be used for patient care. Price competition by insurers to win employer contracts promotes cream-skimming, avoiding subscribers most likely to become patients, and generally minimizes the care that will be insured. Health care just does not fit market prerequisites for cost control any better than it does for ensuring access.

One economic-model reform that makes sense and should not harm quality of care seems almost too simple: Let all the insurers and corporate payers agree on a set of claim forms, billing codes, and other pieces of the proliferating paper blizzard. Even if we do not act to achieve the greater administrative savings possible in a single-track national insurance system, we are not really compelled to stick with the boggling diversity of paperwork that now prevails.

Although doctors tend to decry the economic approach to cost control, one financial incentive factor they have eagerly latched onto is tort reform. This means changing the legal system to set limits on jury awards in malpractice cases, thus reducing malpractice insurance premiums. Yet such insurance causes only 4 percent of costs (though fear of suits may lead to 20 percent of costs through the practice of "defensive" medicine). Furthermore, the basic medical ethic of doing all that one can to help a patient is very firmly embedded in law as well, and courts tend to expect that resources that have a reasonable potential for helping a patient will be used. Tort reform may limit jury awards but will not of itself change the legal-normative value judgments that lead to the practice of defensive medicine.

The Governmental Approach: Mostly Compensation Controls

If I were a physician, I would suspect that the national government is trying desperately in the 1990s to make up for its earlier failure to control provider reimbursement effectively. As we have seen, a host of acronyms summarizes the present scene—DRG, RVS, PPS and VPS, and even PPP (Participating Physician Program). Increasingly tight limits are being placed on balance billing (charges beyond the amount covered by the insurer). Medicare beneficiaries are being encouraged to enroll in HMOs. These are all ways to move the lever of control from the hands of providers to those of payer-regulators.

The landmark development in this control system is the DRG, begun in 1983 and intended to give hospitals a strong internal efficiency incentive by establishing set fees for diagnosed conditions. What has been its financial effect? The increase rate of aggregate Medicare reimbursement for inpatient treatment has been slowed markedly, from an average annual increase of 17 percent in the six years preceding DRGs to 6.1 percent in the first six years after their adoption. However, from 1985 through 1990, Medicare reimbursement to hospitals for outpatient care, not regulated by DRGs, increased 17 percent a year. Pushed in at one end, the hospital pillow bulged at the other, although not as far, so there was a net decrease overall. Now the Bush administration is considering extending the DRG system of prospective payment to outpatient services, setting the same charge (based on usual hospital costs) for each of 297 sets of outpatient services.

The savings to date from DRGs, although not enough to please Medicare officials and Congress, have squeezed hospitals to the point at which it is estimated that the aggregate DRG operating margin for hospitals was *minus* 6.6 percent by 1991 and that 57 percent of all hospitals were on the loss side of their DRG accounts.

Thus prospective payment is an example of cost-saving for the Medicare payer but of cost-shifting for the system as a whole. Hospitals have to raise prices to other buyers, and those buyers then increase their premium demands upon subscribers. To the extent that DRGs actually control costs, it should be said that their influence does extend beyond Medicare, because other payers are also using them. The Kaiser HMO system uses them for managerial oversight by comparing its hospitals' costs per DRG case. Managers of their higher-cost facilities find out how others achieve lower costs and then apply those lessons to their own operations.

In the physician sector (Medicare's Part B), too, government is pushing prospective payment through the fee-schedule/volume-performance-standard (RVS-VPS) system now being introduced. (This is a public utility-style price-control system, of course; so much for the administration's promarket rhetoric.) Effects cannot yet be measured, but if the volume controls work, this approach is almost certain to be more cost-effective than traditional reimbursement. When one considers that physician income in a recent five-year period rose 30 percent compared with 16.3 percent for all other workers, it is easy to see why the physician sector is a target area for Medicare cost-containment efforts. But note also that demand for nurses and some other health care professionals who are in shorter supply than physicians will continue to require compensation increases. Also, the successful experience of Canada and Germany with fee schedules is cited in support of hopeful expectations. But those countries' fee schedules cover most physicians, not just one program among many. This difference may also mean we can expect efforts to impose cost-shifting increases on non-Medicare patients, though such efforts will be counteracted by private-sector programs that adopt the RVS formulas.

It is worth noting as an illustration of the gaps so often left by piece-by-piece approaches to problems that volume controls encourage physicians to shift laboratory tests on their office patients to hospital labs, thus lessening the apparent dollar volume of services being provided simply because hospital-provided outpatient lab services lie outside the data-collecting scope of the system. In neatly symmetrical fashion, imposition of DRGs led hospitals to urge attending physicians to accomplish more of their testing prior to the patient being admitted so that the lab fees could be charged outside the DRG!

The picture of governmental buck-passing to private employers and out-of-pocket payers is even more dismal when one cranks in Medicaid's cost-control efforts. In a classic "good news–bad news" situation, states have responded to expanded federal mandates for pregnant women and young children with two counterproductive measures. One is payments to providers far below hospital costs or the level needed to induce participation by physicians; the other is ever-tighter income restrictions for eligibility of those not mandated for special coverage. The AHA estimates the "Medicaid shortfall" (i.e., costs beyond reimbursement) at $4.3 billion in 1989, requiring that much more cost-shifting to other payers; and Medicaid pays physicians only 69 percent of Medicare rates.

A secondary level of governmental cost controls—one whose savings may not simply be cost-shifted—consists of using HMOs (voluntarily in Medicare; compulsorily in some Medicaid programs) and utilization review. Despite hard effort by the Reagan administration, only about 1 million Medicare patients have enrolled in HMOs, and it is not certain that Medicare saves money even on them. About 2.5 million Medicaid enrollees are also reported to be in HMOs and other managed-care arrangements. In trying to control utilization, Medicare requires that some procedures be done on an outpatient basis and uses Professional Review Organizations (PROs), not-for-profit organizations that contract to examine both cost and quality in hospital practice. Although some reports have indicated lowered utilization rates on procedures that are thought to have been overdone, PROs have not been very successful on either the cost or the quality front.

The Business Approach: Managed Care

In the private sector, insurers and employers try to control costs mostly by embracing the "managed-care" concept. The essence is that the third-party payer does not just pay the bills; it helps decide what bills to pay. Financial and medical considerations are directly and immediately related to one another—reversing the kind of separation that physicians and patients prefer: Do whatever will help the patient and let someone else worry about paying for it.

Managed care is not a precise term, but we can use the Health Insurance Association of America's statement of its common elements:

- Arrangements with selected providers to furnish a comprehensive set of health care services to members
- Explicit standards for the selection of health care providers
- Formal programs for ongoing quality assurance and utilization review
- Significant financial incentives for members to use providers and procedures covered by the plan

More concretely, managed care usually means an HMO or PPO form of organization using providers who have contracted to discount (typically by 10–30 percent) normal charges.

What makes the care itself "managed," and not just the financial arrangements, is the heavy use of utilization review, which lies at the heart of payer intrusion into the patient-physician-hospital relationship. UR includes second-opinion programs (review by a second physician of the first one's decision to perform a particular procedure); prehospital certification (plan approval of both admission and length of stay before one becomes an inpatient); specifications that certain procedures be done only on an outpatient basis; gatekeeping (approval of a primary-care physician before one can use a specialist's services); and limited reimbursement for a service option chosen by the plan managers from among a number of benefit options, such as care provided in a hospital, a nursing home, a board and care facility, or at home.

Increasingly, patients with long-term, high-cost conditions (such as low-weight premature babies and persons with cancer, heart ailments, AIDS, and substance abuse or mental health problems) are assigned case managers. Appropriate utilization is harder to measure in most such areas, creating a special niche within UR. In this most personalized form of managed care, an agent of the plan is assigned to help the patient and physician find the most cost-effective (one hopes not simply the least costly) mode of treatment and provide continuing oversight of the patient's progress. Special networks of providers with good track records are also part of such managed care for mental health and substance abuse cases.

Although case management has many critics, a legitimate need for such close review seems to be warranted by "bad apple" situations, such as those involving psychiatric hospitals that are alleged to have sent out bounty hunters to find well-insured patients and then to have kept them hospitalized until the day their insurance ran out. Southern California Edison, using Prudential as the administrator, emphasizes this form of managed-care because it found that 85 percent of its health expenditures went to handle 15 percent of the cases.

Although UR is mostly designed to avoid possible overutilization (care that is not needed or being ordered more than necessary), managed-care programs sometimes also contain features designed to be positive incentives to more healthy life-styles: physical fitness facilities and wellness programs at the workplace, or lower cost-sharing (sometimes even cash rewards) for employees who maintain an appropriate body weight, or do aerobic exercises, or quit smoking.

Managed-care plans have been developed by HMOs, hospitals, groups of physicians, and insurance companies, with the latter currently being very aggressive in putting together networks and selling their services to employers. Even when the employer self-insures, an insurance company may be used as a contractor to operate its own network and UR system on behalf of the payer.

Prudential Insurance Company, for example, does managed care and claims-processing for more than 100,000 people in northern New Jersey. A company executive, although acknowledging that it costs money to save money, predicts that savings will increase as the plans become more sophisticated. (He also predicts that employers will seek further savings by placing greater burdens on both patients and doctors: patients, by reimbursing only when providers in the network are used; doctors, by paying them on a capitation rather than fee-for-service basis. That's not managed care so much as manipulated finance.)

How widely are managed-care plans being used? Very—and more so every day. In addition to HMOs, which cover 36.5 million people, PPOs have been mushrooming since the 1980s and are now available to about the same number of people. They are probably growing faster than HMOs because insurance companies eagerly put together networks of discounting providers in order to obtain employer contracts.

Advocates who take the HMO figure as showing the wave of the future should note that the rate of increase in HMO membership has slowed down despite employer pressures. And HMO membership is not spreading at all evenly across the country. Half the members are in just eight population centers and almost one-fifth in Kaiser Permanente's California group alone. In only eight states do HMOs include more than 20 percent of the population.

As of 1988, only 28 percent of employees still had indemnity coverage with free choice of provider at no financial penalty. That was down from 41 percent just a year earlier and is presumably even lower today. And UR is being adopted by indemnity plans as much as by the other kinds of plans, so being on an indemnity plan does not mean escaping all of managed care's grasp. An A. Foster Higgins survey in 1990 reported that 93 percent of responding firms were using UR.

There's no doubt therefore that some forms of managed care are growing rapidly. But does it save money for the health care system? In the A. Foster Higgins survey, 64 percent of the firms did not know if their utilization review was cutting costs. The data to assess most aspects of UR and managed care simply do not yet exist, but the degree of effectiveness may not match the degree of popularity.

For one thing, the discounts squeezed from providers will simply encourage more cost-shifting by those providers onto their patients with traditional indemnity plans. And as long as PPOs lack volume controls, the discounts may not do much. Another problem is that UR and case-by-case oversight carry with them the proliferation of different paperwork requirements from a burgeoning variety of entrepreneurial firms contracting to do UR for insurers and employers, thus increasing the already appallingly high administrative overhead of health care. For example, in Prudential's northern New Jersey program, the hands-on activities require eighteen nurses and four part-time medical directors to review treatments proposed by physicians—not to mention the time of office physicians on the phone with UR representatives and the extra clerical burdens imposed on providers' offices.

The biggest cost-saving dimension of managed care is the finding of more than a decade ago that HMOs had substantially lower rates of hospitalization. But that was in staff- and group-model HMOs that had their own facilities, salaried physicians, and a strong nonprofit ethos. The profit-oriented loose networks developed in recent years lack most of the features that gave HMOs their cost advantage. Furthermore, self-contained HMOs, in the currently wasteful mode of private competition, become hybrids and allow patients to select outside providers while still receiving some reimbursement; thus they start to lose the controls they once had. And as medicine generally moves increasingly away from hospitalization, it is not clear what other distinctive feature might enable HMOs to keep their competitive edge.

In utilization review, the longest-standing controls (prehospital certification and second opinions) have changed few decisions from what they would otherwise have been, though adding to costs; review of the number of inpatient days, however, has made a difference. Meaningful UR that is not medically arbitrary presumes the existence of a substantial body of clinically proven practice guidelines; but we are only beginning to develop those. Although some systems use the best guidelines now available, one fears that much UR necessarily tends toward an arbitrary preference for the lowest possible utilization because adequate medical data are not available. As noted earlier regarding managed care's by-product impacts, the reversal of incentives in all capitated systems creates a temptation to underdeliver care, and the restrictions on coverage in many managed-care–UR plans tend to limit access. DRGs and their equivalents in the private sector have also created great tension between hospitals and physicians, as the latter demand services for their patients and the former worry about exceeding insurer-allowed cost limits. Some of that tension is healthy; some makes it harder for physicians to function professionally.

Perhaps overreacting, perhaps not, one hospital executive in 1990 evaluated managed care in a strongly negative fashion: "As far as I'm concerned, managed care is a crock. I can see no value added in what these plans purport to accomplish. Managed care has been tremendously disruptive in patient-physician relationships and in physician referral patterns. In short, I think the way patient care is managed adds to health care costs."[1]

Three fundamental problems limit the long-term potential of all the managed-care rubrics, rules, and regulations:

- Each plan affects only a little piece of the system, often creating its own savings by increasing someone else's costs; thus it has no real leverage on the costs of the system as a whole.

- Utilization review does not directly address high-technology advances at the most meaningful point: decisions regarding their introduction and diffusion on the basis of cost-effectiveness compared with existing treatment modes.

- Managed care does nothing to affect directly the most problematic of all factors in determining overall health care costs—the
  ethos of "do something" medicine. We, the public, tend to
  focus on access to cures more than on living healthier lives to
  avoid the need for cure.

All of these disadvantages lead us to switch from the economic to
the medical model for controlling costs.

The Medical Model: Making the Practice of Medicine More (Cost) Effective

Unlike the economic model of cost control, the medical approach
rests not on a formal body of theory but on a much looser, more
sociological—even partly intuitive—understanding of the state of
the medical arts and the practical workings of health care at the
bedside. It has a variety of dimensions.

Its primary thrust as a cost-controlling strategy takes off from the
basic fact of uncertainty in the art of medicine. It pins its faith on
the hypothesis that research can move art closer to science, thus
increasing certainty in diagnosis and treatment. The financial corollary is that by providing physicians with reliable guidelines for when
to use what, multibillion-dollar savings in hospital days, physician
fees, medications, and so on, can be achieved.

Closely related to practice guidelines is the concept of technology
assessment, looking at the cost and effectiveness of the tools in the
physician's black bag—the "black bag" now being an immense figu-
rative warehouse of equipment, procedures, and organizational
forms.

Quite another kind of effort is the increasingly important phenomenon of self-initiated, patient-determined explicit limits on
treatment—which could be seen as enlarging the concept of medical
appropriateness to include the patient's desires.

In yet another strategy, medically informed assessments of the
health care system's resource needs are combined with economic
concepts to produce plans for regulating the amount of specified
types of resources (e.g., hospital beds) that need to be made
available.

Let's look at some of these approaches in more detail.

Practice Guidelines: The Doctor's Cookbook

For more than two decades, medical researchers have reported finding great variations in the rates of certain treatments undergone by very similar patients in closely comparable communities:

- Of women reaching the age of 70, 20 percent of those in one Maine community had undergone a hysterectomy versus 70 percent in another.

- In two Vermont communities, a pioneering study found that on the basis of three years' experience, the projected tonsillectomy rate by age 20 would be 60 percent in one and 8 percent in the other.

- With similar populations, and health care in both places influenced by university medical centers, Boston and New Haven had a 2-to-1 difference in average inpatient care costs for 1982—$899 versus $451, without measurable difference in the quality of results. The financial implication is substantial: If Boston had treated patients according to New Haven's pattern, its patients (or their payers) would have been saved $300 million that year.

What lies behind such substantial variations? Uncertainty is the primary answer. Despite the very real wonders of modern medicine, the scientific knowledge base for clinical judgments remains fragmentary in many areas. Consequently, the medical profession is without consensus on what to do for many conditions. The impact on variations is shown, in reverse, by Wennberg's finding that practice variation is at its lowest where there is a professional consensus on the preferred approach. Where uncertainty is greatest, what causes a high rate in one area, a low one in another? Wennberg calls it the "practice style factor"—subjective aspects of individual physician attitudes. Similarly, Eddy writes that "the tendency to follow the pack is the most important single explanation of regional variations in medical practice." And he warns that existing uncertainties make clinical judgment a "slippery terrain" for all physicians.[2]

Adding to the problem of inexplicable variations in practice is the overuse of some major procedures. For example, a RAND study of surgery on Medicare patients concluded that almost a third of carotid endarterectomies (cleaning out a major artery) and 14–30 percent of coronary bypasses had been done inappropriately.

Looking on the bright side, we at least have less uncertainty of clinical appropriateness now than was shown in a now-classic 1934 study of tonsillectomies among 1,000 11-year-olds. After 65 percent of 1,000 11-year-olds had had their tonsils removed, the rest were sent to a group of physicians, and 45 percent of them were judged to need the operation. Approximately the same thing happened when those now left over were sent to another set of doctors. After that, they ran out of physicians to continue the study.

A secondary factor in rates of variation appears to be the differing availability of resources. Part of the conventional wisdom is "Roemer's Law": Hospitalization rates will vary in direct ratio with the number of beds. This is part of what Wennberg found in his New Haven–Boston study. Similarly, where there are more specialists, there are more consultations and more hospital visits. Thus the capital resources of an area are a significant factor in health care utilization and costs.

From all such findings has arisen a powerful movement to reduce uncertainty by using research to produce practice guidelines (also called protocols and parameters). In this context "research" means not so much laboratory science as statistical studies of patient outcomes, clinical trials, and reviews of patterns of treatment by panels of experts.

A number of programs to produce clinical guidelines for physicians to rely upon in making treatment choices have been going on for some years. Included are the consensus conferences of the National Institutes of Health, the Clinical Efficacy Project of the American College of Physicians, AMA reviews of standards with its related specialty associations, AMA-RAND cooperative development of medical appropriateness standards; and the outcomes management studies inaugurated in the private sector by Dr. Paul M. Ellwood in the late 1980s. Finally, partly because national legislators seized upon the variations studies as a promising focal point for medically effective cost-control efforts, Congress in 1989 reorganized earlier on-again, off-again efforts into an Agency for Health Care Policy and Research (AHCPR) and gave it meaningful financing—$102 million for fiscal 1992, for example.

AHCPR sponsors research to develop scientific information about the clinical effectiveness of different diagnostic and treatment strategies for a variety of conditions. Along with other information, the results are used by panels of experts (and some patient-consumers, too) to develop clinically relevant guidelines. AHCPR defines these as "systematically developed statements to assist practitioner and patient decisions about appropriate health care for specific clinical circumstances." Because about 40 illnesses account for 70 percent of nonsurgical hospital admissions, and just 23 operations cover 60 percent of major surgical admissions, there is a considerable potential for significant gains in reducing unnecessary treatment costs without having to wait until every condition and every treatment have been evaluated. AHCPR's first five guidelines, scheduled for early 1992, cover postoperative pain, pressure sores (e.g., bedsores), urinary incontinence, cataracts, and depression. Sickle-cell anemia, AIDS, lower back pain, and mammogram screening are probably the next areas for development.

Once guidelines exist, what then? How do they get put into practice? That part—involving physician egos and patient demands—may prove harder than deciding on the appropriate conditions for a treatment. Publication in medical journals will almost certainly not be sufficient to achieve widespread adoption; and edicts by Medicare or private insurers would certainly lead to a physician rebellion against enforced "cookbook medicine." Success will have to come from compromise innovations.

Among the earliest efforts was one twenty years ago in which Wennberg persuaded the Vermont medical society to circulate information about tonsillectomy variations to hospitals in the state. Two practicing physicians in a high-rate area took the ball from there, tightened standards, and achieved a decline of 90 percent of their area's earlier rate. Now Medicare has begun a program called Comparative Performance Reports in which a physician's use of specific services for Medicare patients will be compared with the statistical norm for others in the same specialty and locality. The 1 percent who most exceed the norm will receive letters and comparative data so they can see for themselves how they stand in relation to their peers in the same locality. The hope is that lower rates (hence lower costs to Medicare) will result.

State and local medical societies will have to play major dissemination roles, as we know that informal peer pressure can have a significant impact. But they and others will need innovative dissemination materials. Wennberg has developed a prostate surgery videodisc, for example, that doctors and patients can view to aid in jointly determining which alternative treatment to use. And some of RAND's research on appropriateness has been made available to insurers in the form of privately marketed software.

Of course the computer will play a role—some doctors fear too great a role. In one experiment for diagnosing heart attacks in patients arriving in emergency rooms with chest pains, a computer program derived from analyzing over 1,000 case histories was tested against nearly 5,000 other cases treated by physicians. The result: For patients not having heart attacks, the physicians correctly diagnosed 71 percent of the cases, the computer model 74 percent. For those who did have heart attacks, it was a tie. Going by the computer in all cases would have avoided 11.5 percent of coronary intensive care admissions—and care delivered in ICUs is almost four times as expensive as in general care units. Arguing that guidelines are a proper response to the explosion of medical information that confronts busy doctors, Brook foresees a time when every physician will have on the desk a computer with recommendations for appropriate treatments for a host of conditions. He suggests that professionally authenticated standards will not only help doctors and their patients as individuals but they may have several favorable effects on the health care system as a whole when physician compliance can be used

- By PPOs to select providers, instead of just picking those offering the lowest price
- By payers to determine appropriate reimbursement policies
- By medical licensing bodies for relicensing
- By the court system in establishing practice expectations in malpractice cases.

Overall, Brook has estimated that greater assurance of the appropriateness of treatments might conceivably reduce system costs by $50 billion a year.

The greatest advantage of guidelines is that they will be used by doctors to choose the most cost-effective treatment *on medical grounds*, that is, by exercising professional judgment—not (like most current UR) imposed on doctors by payers exercising mostly financial criteria. In fact, some of the early guidelines are already being incorporated into insurance company UR procedures. Hopefully, medically proven guidelines will in time be able to inform all utilization screening, thus legitimizing UR by turning it into a tool used by doctors that happens to save payers money, rather than a payer's tool that hassles doctors and threatens the primacy of the patient's needs in determining treatment.

It sounds great, but there are some problems.

Aside from the problems of getting doctors' attention and changing their behavior (and it is no small challenge to tell an experienced professional that he or she should change the way things are done), the guidelines themselves promote skepticism. For one thing, research may show that some procedures should receive more use rather than less. For another, to permit doctors to take individual patient differences into account, guidelines may have to be so broad that they will affect only a small proportion who are operating entirely outside of existing informal standards. And a standard developed today may be outmoded tomorrow because of technological change. Can revisions made in a cumbersome peer evaluation process ever keep up with the pace of scientific change?

Another problem has surfaced in AHCPR's commendable efforts to build a patient perspective into its evaluations. Criteria will have to include not only the direct biomedical effects of a treatment (an organ is repaired; a disease is arrested) but such additional aspects as these: Is the pain relieved? Is the patient's mobility restored? Can the patient now lead a life she herself thinks is worth living?

And Dr. Philip Caper at Dartmouth Medical School cautions that completely persuasive scientific evidence is hard to find and consensus is hard to reach. When strong consensus does exist, the guidelines may not be needed anyway. Far more pessimistic than Brook and other supporters of guidelines, Caper welcomes the improvement in information that guidelines development will produce but says the effort "will not save a nickel."[3] That's probably too pessimistic, but members of Congress hoping for quick and massive cost savings, and physician groups hoping that the promise of guidelines research can be used to stave off harsher economic controls imposed by payers, will almost certainly be disappointed. Guidelines can help medically, and probably economically, but will not be a cost-containment panacea.

Technology Assessment: Are All New Mousetraps Better Mousetraps?

A close relative of guidelines is called technology assessment (TA): examining newly proposed medical technologies (machines, medications, even organizational patterns like ICUs) to determine the value of making them widely available for physician and hospital use, the appropriate conditions for their use, and whether to encourage or discourage payer reimbursement for using them.

With much evidence of too-easy diffusion of very expensive technologies, TA may be one of the most promising medical-model approaches to cost control. William B. Schwartz has pointed out that the pace of technological innovation is a crucial variable because it is much more within medical institutions' control than population growth, the aging of the population, or the prices of goods that have to be purchased in competition with buyers from all other sectors. TA is also a good candidate because there is much greater centralized leverage by payers *before* technological innovations are introduced than after their use becomes routinized.

Technology assessment is far from new. AHCPR's predecessor agencies did about 150 assessments in the 1980s. But as the cost-increasing pace of technological advances seems to quicken ever more—perhaps because advances often mean more complexity, and complexity breeds cost increases—interest by payers in seeing that the advances are worthwhile quickens in tandem. TA is also an essential ingredient in developing practice guidelines, the two being overlapping concepts.

Traditionally, TA has focused on safety and biomedical efficacy; for example, does the test clearly indicate the presence or absence of the suspected disease? In recent years, the criteria have been broadened and the process made more complicated. Now TA is also used to try to estimate final outcomes in terms of personal, economic, and ethical factors such as the patient's ability to function normally, or the cost-effectiveness of the innovation versus some existing technique (tissue plasminogen activator versus streptokinase, for example). Scientists and physicians have to be complemented by economists, ethicians, epidemiologists, and biostatisticians to do rounded assessments today.

Some assessments are sponsored in the private sector; Blue Cross and Blue Shield Association has a significant program. In prescription drugs, much is done by pharmaceutical manufacturers in order to meet Food and Drug Administration demands for safety and efficacy data—which then have to be checked for self-interest bias. Most assessment ends up being a governmental responsibility, however. The individual physician has neither the number of cases nor the epidemiological-statistical training to accomplish meaningful TA. And large-scale evaluations that can be used by everyone will not be paid for by private firms that cannot reap all the benefits. (A case of "positive externalities," in economic jargon, which makes TA an appropriate public function as part of government's obligation to further the common welfare.)

Much of AHCPR's assessment effort is in response to requests from Medicare and CHAMPUS (the Civilian Health and Medical Program of the Armed Forces for military dependents), but the need may have been stimulated initially by a medical-devices manufacturer, a practitioner, or one of the fiscal intermediaries that handle Medicare bills from providers. Completed TAs give the requesting party recommendations for coverage and appropriate use of the technology concerned, and the assessment reports are made publicly available after the program concerned has made its coverage decision. Through such dissemination, the medical—and sometimes financial—benefits of the assessments can be built into the coverage and reimbursement decisions of both public and private payers.

AHCPR's bureaucratic home is in the Public Health Service (where also are located the National Institutes of Health, the Centers for Disease Control, and the Food and Drug Administration), *not* in the Health Care Financing Administration. Its efforts are thus insulated from direct pressures to focus on saving the government money in the clinical application of research. Even though its Office of Health Technology Assessment does recommend whether Medicare should cover a new technology, the fundamental criterion for its recommendations is medical and sometimes financial effectiveness, but not budgetary impact as such.

But what happens when the Health Care Financing Administration (HCFA), using the recommendations but also being responsible for Medicare's fiscal health, makes its reimbursement decisions? The agency has always asserted that it bases reimbursement policy on safety and efficacy, but there have long been suspicions of a hidden cost-containment agenda when decisions on expensive technologies are denied or long delayed. Medicare labeled balloon angioplasty for dilating arteries experimental, and therefore nonreimbursable, even after the FDA said it was safe and effective. It took a lawsuit by a patient to move Medicare on that one. HCFA tentatively proposed in early 1989 to add cost-effectiveness frankly and explicitly to its coverage criteria but is apparently still some distance from publishing a final version of the new regulation. If added, the new criterion would likely not be used in a coverage decision about a breakthrough technology for which nothing comparable is available but would be applied to something of marginal effectiveness yet expensive compared with alternatives.

The very "big ticket" technology of PET scanners is treated as experimental and not reimbursable under Medicare at this time. An AHCPR evaluation is reportedly well under way, but no time for completion has been set. That assessment, and HCFA's reimbursement decision based on it, may well determine PET's fate, for its high cost makes it unlikely to be widely installed unless Medicare reimbursement can be counted on. (And that decision will also largely determine private insurance reimbursement policy.) When the cost is not so great, however, as with tissue plasminogen activator (TPA), physician determination to make use of it seems to have overridden Medicare's decision not to increase the DRG payment for the procedures in which it is used, even though it will add thousands to treatment costs.

Medicare may have a hard time making cost-effectiveness decisions stick, at least when a group of physicians takes a strong stand in conjunction with lobbying by the medical-devices trade group, the Health Industry Manufacturers Association. But the pressures may never have a chance to develop if Medicare says no to reimbursement before a new technology gets started. Most of the obstacles facing practice guidelines will also apply to TA, so its cost-containing contribution is also not likely to be as great as the wishful thinking of budget-buffeted politicians would make it.

We should not forget that technological advances can sometimes have money-*saving* impacts. By sharply reducing hospitalization time, the general use of antibiotics a generation ago became a major cost-controlling agent. Technological advancements made it possible to close most tuberculosis sanitariums; polio research has paid off tremendously, both medically and financially. Currently, overuse of hysterectomies by 30 percent or more has been asserted; some have been performed simply to end minimal bleeding. But recently the Food and Drug Administration has approved use of a tool for endometrial ablation (i.e., removing the uterine lining) that costs much less and means an easier time for the patient.

There is no reason why the government's criteria for sponsoring health care research could not give priority to work that focuses on cost-saving technologies—perhaps even to a special subprogram with research grant incentives. We have to acknowledge, though, that getting biomedical scientists as interested in the goal of cost-effective medicine as in getting credit for the next miracle will be hard to do, especially with about $8 billion annually in the National Institutes of Health research budget oriented to finding cures for cancer, stroke, Alzheimer's disease, and others. And would any of us want it otherwise? Yet a budget of $8 billion would seem to permit room for subsidizing some work to devise technologies that reduce costs of treatment.

Does this evaluation leave ambiguity in its wake? It should, for the effort to use technology assessment in a cost-effectiveness context is too new and involves too many conflicting pressures and incentives to warrant any clear prediction about the size of its potential contribution to solving health care's financial crisis. But we can surely expect it to be at least a significant counterweight to all the marketing efforts by manufacturers to get physicians to use innovations beyond their areas of proven cost-effectiveness.

A Grab Bag of Additional Ways to Contain Costs

Guidelines and technology assessment are the most prominent modes of cost containment in the medical model. But a number of other possible contributors should be briefly mentioned.

Alternative delivery systems (ADSs) is a phrase often used to summarize ways of organizing medical care more efficiently than through single-office FFS practitioners. HMOs and PPOs were once the prime examples, but both are now so common that they have to be considered mainstream rather than alternatives. Another kind of group practice is done in the 650 federally supported Community and Migrant Health Centers in 200 free clinics and in other not-for-profit clinics. These alternatives promote better health while saving money. Such clinics greatly reduce use of expensive hospital emergency room treatment as a substitute for primary care, and their patients less often need hospitalization than do similar patients not able to use such clinics. Unlike most mainline providers, clinics tend to be located where their patients live, and they establish a close relationship with a social services network, a combination that probably creates one of the nation's better examples of a true safety net.

A related example of a cost-effective alternative is provided by a family-oriented maternity center in Philadelphia that is staffed mostly by certified nurse midwives. In addition to having lower personnel costs than an all-M.D. clinic, this center had a caesarian birthrate 2.5 times lower than in the teaching hospital with which it was affiliated—and without any negative medical consequences.

Here are some additional alternatives that might save money while maintaining—sometimes even improving—the quality of care:

1. Regionalization of high-tech, high-cost hospital procedures. Balloon angioplasties, heart and kidney transplants, and similarly complex surgical procedures are expensive in both equipment needs and the personnel costs of teams that include physicians and a number of technicians. Their proliferation beyond the number needed in a community when utilized on a full-time basis has been stimulated by interhospital competition. This wastes millions of dollars in duplicative facilities. More importantly, it is medically dangerous, because experts agree that a significant volume of cases is essential for the maintenance of the required skills.

In a 1990 survey, nearly half of California hospitals doing coronary angioplasty did not perform the minimum number recommended by the appropriate specialty societies. Where competition was strongest, in Los Angeles and Orange counties, the proportion below the quality-related minimum approached two-thirds. Although government programs to limit overcapacity were a casualty of the 1980s fever for deregulation, in the 1990s an increasing number of private insurers are responding to this situation with their own measures to steer their heart surgery and organ transplant patients to selected regional centers that have good rates and ensure better care.

2. More use of nurse practitioners (NPs) and physician assistants (PAs). Research covering over a quarter-century has shown that these "physician extenders" provide high-quality care, yet their training costs are lower than for physicians, as are their salaries. One physician, Dr. Mark R. Depman, who has worked in an inner city clinic where he found excellent care being provided mostly by NPs, has suggested that perhaps nursing schools should be the primary training grounds for general practitioners, leaving only the training of specialists and researchers to the medical schools. NPs and PAs may have a special impact in future years as the nursing-home population grows. (Readers who have served in any of the armed forces will

remember that most treatment was provided by the medical corps and may wonder, as I often have, why greater use has not been made of such paraprofessionals in civilian life.)

3. Hospices—places where the terminally ill receive comforting medication (but no curative efforts) and generally greater peace than is possible in a hospital—are both more humane and less expensive for awaiting death with dignity when death is diagnostically certain. Hospices will be used more as they become better known and as more patients declare their desire to avoid useless treatment.

4. Emphasizing preventive medicine. If prevention were more broadly included in insurance coverage, much curative medicine would not be needed. Just when the reduced treatment would exceed the cost of added preventive measures is impossible to measure, but it does seem safe to say that an expenditure on prevention greater than the present proportion of three-tenths of 1 percent of health care expenditures would pay off, in health *and* money.

Lesser steps for controlling costs—but ones that can cumulatively make a difference—include use of generic drugs when filling prescriptions except in cases where the physician has a medical reason for insisting on the name brand, and building more cost awareness into medical school training—and into the continuing medical education of physicians already in practice, so that a whole generation is not skipped in being sensitized.

In short, if we start with medical rather than financial objectives, a great deal can be done to simultaneously improve the quality of care, use more effectively whatever we do spend, and sometimes actually save money. All of these approaches are preferable to the emphasis on cost-shifting and cost-cutting of the economic model, which could turn medical care from a profession into a competitive bottom-line industry not basically different from the world of used car sales.

Partial Controls Are Good—But Not Good Enough

Where do we come out after looking at all of the cost-controlling measures and programs discussed so far? Would they make a dent in the metainflationary escalation of health care expenditures? Assuredly, yes.

Would it be enough to stabilize costs at or near the rate of increase of GNP, or of wage and salary increases? Almost assuredly not, because each of them acts only on one element of the system. They are all *partial* controls when the essence of effective control is to find *overall* or *global* controls. If we don't cap the system as a whole, money will continue to ooze through the cracks left between the separate control points. So let's move on now to approaches that can affect the entire system.

7
Cutting Costs: Overall Approaches

There are two major possibilities for achieving overall control of costs. One involves change in the values and expectations held by the two parties most threatened by payer dominance, physicians and their patients. The other centers on capacity controls: limiting the allocations for health care as one among many claimants to society's resources.

Patients and Doctors

The attitudes, expectations, and actions of these primary parties, and their relationship with one another, will crucially affect what can be done to reduce costs while maintaining quality care.

How We Patient-Payers Can Help Ourselves

We sometimes forget—especially if well covered by a third-party payer—that in the aggregate we patients are also prominent payers in the system, providing about 28 percent of total health care expenditures. As employers shift more and more of their costs to us, it becomes increasingly in our own interest to be prudent in using health care.

The most effective way to be prudent is to avoid the need for care whenever possible. How? By adopting life-style behavior patterns that maintain or help develop good health status.

The right choices regarding smoking, diet, the use of alcohol, exercise (and yes, safe sex) can do more for our health and financial well-being than all the expensive curative medicine our researchers and specialists can come up with. Secretary of Health and Human Services Louis W. Sullivan has made self-responsibility for good health his major theme, pointing out that preventable deaths from smoking (now over 400,000 annually) account for 87 percent of all deaths from lung cancer and for 21 percent from heart disease. Smoking by pregnant women is responsible for 20–30 percent of low birth weights. Death and disability from smoking cost $52 billion a year. Alcohol is involved in half the highway deaths and 40 percent of drownings and is the leading cause of cirrhosis of the liver.

Sullivan says it is time to stop using the medical system "as a fix-it shop for our sloppy life-styles."[1] Happily, we do as a nation seem to have been making progress in the right direction. Death rates from heart disease and stroke went down in the 1980s, thanks partly to medications but mostly to life-style changes: reduced overall smoking rates and diets lower in fats and cholesterol.

Promoting good health habits and providing preventive services clearly can reduce many costs while making us a more fit nation—an excellent example of the medical-model approach to cost containment.

Yet there are caveats to express even here. Some prevention and screening programs for early detection of diseases cost much more than they will save. Even exercise has an economic downside in the price of belonging to faddish health clubs and spas—not to mention the resultant growth of spending for the services of sports medicine clinics! And lives saved and extended by better habits will sometimes be affected by problems such as senility that earlier deaths avoid. But surely our values will support spending more toward the end of a normal life span than on earlier repairs of abused bodies.

Efforts are also under way to increase patient self-responsibility and reduce costs by simplifying the provision of basic information to individuals. The Harvard Community Health Plan, a large HMO, is testing a computerized service that answers basic health care questions (such as "I have a runny nose, a fever of 101, and cold sweats; what's wrong with me? What should I do to help myself?") through an interactive computerized phone system. An entrepreneurial medical information line makes basic information about more than 300 medical topics (for example, diarrhea, sinusitis, Parkinson's disease, colon cancer) available through a 900 phone number; the information is approved by the American Academy of Family Physicians Foundation. Not world shaking, but a promising development.

An example of the need for information and the vital importance of responsible behavior that I found striking and startling is this:

Although the most frequently cited indicator of low-birth-weight babies is poverty and its concomitant lack of health care access, cigarette smoking by pregnant women turns out to be more important. The smokers are three times as likely as nonsmokers to have at-risk babies.

We are taking better care of ourselves; we are also rethinking our traditional deference to medical providers and the do-everything ethic. An increasing (if still small) number of people are insisting on sharing actively in decisions about what health care they want and do not want, from asking whether one more test will really accomplish anything (see Morris B. Abram anecdote in this chapter) to insisting on patient rights and more active use of the doctrine of informed consent. Not exactly "participatory democracy," but certainly part of our society's general movement away from giving experts and specialists carte blanche to decide what's good for us.

I do not mean to suggest that patient autonomy be used to turn health care into just another commodity whose supply simply responds to consumer demand. The objective of a health care system is good health, not consumer satisfaction. So there will be expenditures that the insurance we all share in paying for, publicly or privately, should not cover—such as diagnostic tests used only to please the patient, or purely cosmetic surgeries that Medicare recently decided it would no longer cover. Such consumer satisfaction use of health care, when without a medical professional's judgment that the service will improve health status, should be like all other consumer expenditures: an out-of-pocket responsibility of the person wanting them. In fact, perhaps doctors who order lab tests just to please or reassure patients, although knowing that they will not affect the treatment decision, should share the cost out of *their* pockets as an incentive against providing medically unnecessary care!

There are practical limits to this idealistic position, of course. For example, a suggestion that just will not be accepted in our society of middle-class expectations—and in an era of every hospital trying to attract more patients—would be to reduce sharply the level of amenities. Get rid of TV sets, phones by every bedside, electrical beds, wide menu choices, and semiprivate accommodations as the hospital board-and-room standards. Much money could be saved, and other nations do offer more spartan surroundings; but it is not likely to happen here, except in facilities for those who have no choice in

---

Improving the Doctor-Patient Relationship

Morris B. Abram is an attorney who has served as president of Brandeis University and as chairman, 1981–1983, of the President's Commission for the Study of Ethical Problems in Medicine and Behavioral Research. The following is excerpted from his comments on experiences he had after having been treated for leukemia.

I have become an extremely wary user of medical service, although I am extremely grateful for it, and I have no doubt that we have the finest medical system in the world. . . . But the fact is, the doctor-patient relationship has broken down. . . .

Let me give you this illustration. I have not seen an oncologist in five years, but I went to see an ordinary internist, a marvelous person. I was terribly impressed with him. The other day, he said to me, "Morris, you've got a murmur in your right aortic valve."

I am 67. I said, "What am I supposed to do about it?"

"Nothing."

"Is it going to hurt me?"

"No, I don't think so. It's going to outlast you, anyway."

"Shall I stop doing anything?"

"No, but come back for an echocardiogram in two weeks," he said. "By the way, have you got a dermatologist?"

"Yes."

"Has he seen that brown spot on your ear lobe?"

"I guess so."

"Better let him see it again."

Now, bear in mind that these doctors know of my relationship to the medical field and my interest in it.

---

the matter. So we are quite unlikely to escape the values of consumerism completely.

Advance Directives

The spread of statutes authorizing *living wills* and *durable powers of attorney for health care* is becoming a major vehicle for expressing the more autonomous role of patients. Living wills (legal in almost all states) are a way of giving directions in advance of becoming ill about what limits we want placed on care if we become too incapacitated to speak for ourselves at a later time. Because we cannot specify in advance all the circumstances that might arise, the more flexible instrument of a durable power is gaining adherents. In the more flexible instrument, one can name another person or persons to act on one's behalf when incapacitated, legally permitting them to exercise their judgment of what we would have wanted done—or not done, as is often the case with use of these powers. These documents are now recognized by statute in almost half the states.

At the end of a week, I called up the internist and said, "I want to ask you a question. It doesn't make any difference to me what that echocardiogram costs. I'm not paying for it, the insurance company is. But I want to know why I've got to spend the time to go down there and get that echocardiogram. Whatever it tells you, are you going to change anything, make any recommendation, or do anything?"

"No."

"Then why in the hell am I having it?"

"Good question. Don't come."

Next I went to see the dermatologist. He looked at my ear lobe and said, "I've seen it. I think it's an angioma, a broken blood vessel, but if your internist thinks . . . ," and he got out his knife.

"Now wait a minute," I said. "I'm going swimming this afternoon."

"Not if I take it out. You're not going swimming for five days."

"Well, now," I said. "That's serious. Can you do a needle biopsy?"

"No," he said, "but I can stick a needle in it and draw back, and if it's an angioma, as I think it is, it'll disappear."

"Why don't you do that?"

He did; and it disappeared.

Now, if this can happen in reputable places with reputable doctors, you can imagine what the costs are to this country as a result of negligence or ignorance or worse.

(Reprinted by permission from Morris B. Abram, "The Individual's Role in Controlling Cost and Quality," in Frank B. McArdle, ed., *The Changing Health Care Market.* Washington, DC: Employee Benefit Research Institute, 1987, pp. 163–164.)

The durable power can be expressed as a general grant of discretion to become operative when one is incapable of giving informed consent, such as in this form authorized in California and distributed by the state medical society: "I hereby grant to my agent full power and authority to make health care decisions for me including the right to consent, refuse consent, or withdraw consent to any care, treatment, service, or procedure." This statement can be combined with special provisions and limitations. The California form provides three statements from which one can choose (or one can write one's own detailed instructions). They range from

I do not want life-sustaining treatment . . . if the burdens of treatment outweigh the expected benefits. I want my agent to consider the relief of suffering and the quality as well as the extent of the possible extension of my life.

through

I want life-sustaining treatment to be provided unless I am in a coma which my doctors reasonably believe to be irreversible.

to

> I want my life to be prolonged to the greatest extent possible without regard to my condition, the chances I have for recovery or the cost of the procedures.

Choice of the first or second alternative—a choice increasingly being made—would fulfill patient desires and also reduce costs for one's insurer, one's family, and the nation's health care system.

Stimulated by stories like the Nancy Cruzan case in which the U.S. Supreme Court upheld a Missouri court decision compelling her family to keep her alive because there was not "clear and compelling evidence" of Nancy's wishes, as required by that state's law, Congress enacted the Patient Self-Determination Act, which requires hospitals and nursing homes to advise patients of any state laws on durable powers and living wills. Even in the Cruzan case, the Supreme Court called a right not to consent to treatment a "logical corollary" of informed consent—so long as the intent has been made clear in advance in a state-approved manner.

A more controversial possible use of advance directives is suggested by recently publicized cases of assisted suicide. This is not, I believe, something that can be legalized simply by inclusion in a patient's statement of treatment desires.

A new medical standard is evolving: When the patient (or surrogate) perceives further treatment as tantamount to prolonging dying rather than as extending life *at a quality acceptable to the patient*, then patient self-determination permits the withdrawal of consent to further treatment. The increasing choice of hospices (where therapeutic efforts are abandoned and emphasis is placed on relief of pain and the provision of comforting surroundings) instead of hospitals by the terminally ill is a significant sign of the new standard's acceptance.

The Changing Culture of Medical Practice

These changes in the rights and roles of patients are paralleled by changes in the culture of medicine, or the ethos of the physician. The "do something" ethic cited earlier as a characteristic of American medical practice has equally been a part of American patient expectations. They go in tandem and must, over time, change in tandem. In the short run, they sometimes collide head-on.

Sharing the same view as physicians, we patients have assumed that we need to preserve the traditional aggressive approach. A brief comparison with Great Britain helps to show there can be other sets of assumptions about the right way to proceed. In her book *Medicine and Culture*, Lynn Payer quotes a British physician who characterizes medical training there as "self-critical. You are taught to question the need for things being done." An American doctor reported that in her own training it was assumed "that the risk of acting is almost always preferable to the risk of not acting. My class in medical school was absorbing the idea that when it comes to tests, technology and interventions, more is better. No one ever talked about the negative aspects of intervention."[2] But note that defining more as better is as much the prevailing view of patients as of doctors.

The traditional differences between Britain and the United States are strikingly apparent in responses to a medical journal article stating that chemotherapy added only a few months to the lives of elderly cancer patients but that it caused severe pain and vomiting. The American authors of the paper, Payer reports, thought the extra time alive made the process worthwhile; British commentators thought not.

Another difference, perhaps even greater today than it was a few years ago, is that the American patient would be much less likely to defer to the doctor's judgment. As far as utilization rates and costs go, this can cut either way. When patients all agreed that extending life was the overriding goal, lack of deference meant demanding that more be done. But in the context of the emerging patient ethos that gives greater weight to quality of life, and so to using denial of consent to forgo unwanted treatment, the U.S. patient may be changing faster than the U.S. doctor. In that case, the effect of the patient's newfound autonomy will be to move the physician in the direction of the British view that not all possible treatment is worth doing—not for financial reasons, but as a matter of outcome values as defined by the patient.

In our conventional unspoken assumptions about living, dying, and the role of medical care, the patient has been seen as having an *obligation* as well as a desire not to die. The "enemy" is death, and medicine is a war. Bioethician Judith Wilson Ross writes of a doctor facing a dying patient: "'Don't crump out on me!' the physician yells in frustration and fear." She says that death will have to be seen as a natural event rather than as the enemy before we will be able to adopt a more sensible approach to the limits of treatment.[3]

Dr. Alexander Leaf looks at our values in terms of how we measure the system's success. He suggests that we replace our expectations for longer life with the goal of maintaining good health for as long as possible but then reducing the application of treatments when they can no longer restore health and normal functioning. That, I think, is one legitimate way in which patients—and physicians as independent professionals—can accept the economics-derived proposition that marginal benefit must exceed marginal cost.

Just how difficult it will be to shift the practice of medicine in such directions is strikingly illustrated by some recent reports on medical decisions regarding premature babies. Although health spending on the aged has received more attention, hospital expenditures on premature babies—and lifetime costs for those who survive greatly disabled—often exceed those on the elderly, sometimes $500,000 even before the child leaves the hospital.

The general trend toward patient rights is contradicted in some cases. Parents are reported to be losing the right to decide when extraordinary means should not be used to "save" a premature baby whose hemorrhaging is almost certain to produce cerebral palsy and severe retardation. Sarah Thorson, mother of a set of triplets, described her experience when one of the newborns had to undergo placement of a shunt to drain excess brain fluid and suffered cardiac arrest. "There was a roomful of doctors around this tiny baby, trying to resuscitate him. After it was over, I looked at the neonatologist and said, 'At what point do we say enough is enough for this little boy?'" The doctor, she said, snapped back, "You don't make those decisions. We do." When another of Sarah Thorson's newborns needed the same procedure, she asked the surgeon to consider not reviving the child if he had a cardiac arrest. The doctor responded, "I'm not your executioner."[4]

Is this simply the traditional medical ethic confronting a distraught parent? No; medical experts see such aggressive treatment as partly a matter of professional challenge—doctors experimenting to see just how far the new technologies can go in keeping smaller and smaller babies alive. The ethical use of technology has not been examined, and professional pride may add up to medical hubris exercised at the financial expense of insurers. Such hubris certainly can exacerbate the agony of parents, who may not be emotionally or financially prepared to meet the lifetime needs of the child after the doctor "succeeds" and the baby leaves the hospital. Changing medical care toward a quality-of-life ethic will not be easy.

In short, whether we are dealing with a simple or a complex decision—whether to do another $100 worth of diagnostic tests or whether to expend resources to provide "curative" treatment to a nonfunctioning patient with a terminal illness—it is not rules, regulations, market forces, financial incentives, or better measures of technological "appropriateness" that will determine most of our choices and the costliness of our health care delivery system. Our decisions will be determined by our sense of values and our understanding of the human condition, its possibilities (of which Americans are culturally always well aware) and its limitations (of which we are generally less aware than the people of other nations).

Patients and doctors together, it turns out, are still at the center of the system. No longer totally dominating the picture, the doctor may welcome the chance to share with the patient the burden of deciding what is medically worth doing in a system of constrained resources. Just how much costs will be contained will then be (as it should) largely a function of the interaction between medical knowledge and the patient's quality-of-life values within the broad, changing, but still basically activist American culture.

Capacity Constraints and Health Care Rationing

What is the best way to combine medical criteria with budgetary limits? This question leads to the following nitty-gritty questions:

1. Will we/can we impose an overall expenditure limit within which medical professionals will be free (they may see it more as forced) to decide which treatments will be used and which forgone?

2. Or will we explicitly ration health care, not only excluding (at least from third-party coverage) the potentially harmful and the therapeutically useless but also refusing some potentially beneficial care to some categories of patients? For example, should we apply a marginal cost-benefit test to procedures that are thought to be beneficial but only marginally so—the test that makes the diagnosis 98 instead of 96 percent certain, or the therapy that will keep a terminally ill patient minimally alive at high cost for three more days or weeks? Should we refuse organ transplants to patients not likely to achieve good quality of life or much longer life even with the transplant?

Expenditure Leverage Through Capacity Controls

All the approaches to cost containment discussed so far share a crucial attribute: They are financially open-ended; they set no overall cap on system expenditures, or even on any single major segment. They will in the aggregate almost certainly reduce the rate of health care inflation from whatever it might otherwise have been. But we don't know by how much, so we don't know whether the savings will be sufficient to satisfy the budgetary imperatives of political and business policymakers.

This is the big difference between the United States and other industrial democracies in the financial dimension of delivery systems. Canada, Great Britain, and Germany (the West German model) vary as much among themselves in their mixtures of local and central decisionmaking and private-public provision of health services as they do collectively from us. Yet they agree on one element of centralization that our traditions of pluralism and institutional autonomy have led us to avoid. That element, in one form or another, is called *global budgeting* (GB). It may be essential for leveraging maximum use of all the other cost-control measures.

Global budgeting is an institutional arrangement that sets an overall expenditure cap (often by a single payer) that is comprehensive in both demographic scope and medical services coverage. At its most effective, GB would involve a single buyer for health care for an entire population. Canada, Britain, and Germany each encompass close to 90 percent of health expenditures within their respective budgetary controls. This is apparently enough to ensure fiscal effectiveness. Each country spends a lower proportion of GNP on health care compared with the United States, yet maintains equivalent indicators of quality.

Global budgeting is the opposite of "open-ended entitlement," which is basically how Medicare, Medicaid, and traditional private indemnity insurance operate. In such entitlement systems, which correlate closely with fee-for-service supply and retroactive reimbursement, the third-party payer knows how large the tab is for a given period of time only after the fact. If you are entitled to the service, the payer may not say, "Sorry, we've run out of funds." This is the open-ended aspect of entitlement, and nothing in all the cost-control approaches mentioned up till now places a lid on it. Global budgeting would.

Let's use Canada to illustrate how the concept works. As noted earlier, Canada is a federation with 10 provinces. Although health care financing began with open-ended 50–50 sharing between the two levels, the national government shifted in 1977 to a specific annual block grant to the provinces, which increases no faster than GNP rises. Because the national government does not reimburse the provinces for a share of each service rendered (as Washington does for state Medicaid programs) and total costs have risen faster than GNP, Ottawa's contribution is now only about 37 percent of total health expenditures and is projected to go a bit lower.

The provinces are thus responsible for the bulk of their health budgets and have substantial autonomy in how they meet their responsibility to supply the national system's package of benefits. If they want to maintain their programs without imposing copayments, they have to meet cost increases beyond GNP out of their own revenues. Ottawa's cap thus provides a strong incentive for the provinces to be cost-effective. Global budgeting for all hospitals is therefore a primary control. On the basis of information regarding the expected number of patients and types of treatment needed, the provincial health minister (secretary of health in our parlance) negotiates with each hospital a total budget for the year. It is up to the administration of each hospital and its physicians to stay within that figure, and they mean business about it. The second major control, over physicians, consists of a fee schedule and bargaining between the provincial medical association and government over the rates per service *and* the total available in a given year for all physician services. If the individual services add up to more than the bargained sum, there is a lowering of reimbursement to recoup the overage. This global budget for doctors' services constitutes a real volume control and produces very hard bargaining, which has, for example, led to a physician strike in Ontario.

With costs rising faster than GNP, the provinces are caught between the national government's GNP cap and the demands of providers and the public, both of which seem to be increasing. The rate of health care expenditure growth is therefore exceeding provincial revenue increases. Ontario, for example, had a 10-year cost increase of 63 percent while its economy grew by 43 percent. With provincial global budgeting for hospitals and physician fee pools being the result of annual negotiations and not, as at the national level, legally constrained by the rate of GNP growth, the strength of provider group pressures is apparently too great to hold a firm line at the provincial level. And now the national government has frozen its contribution through 1995, perhaps turning a serious problem for the provinces into a crisis. So even Canada is now having political trouble trying to hold the line on costs, which diminishes somewhat the earlier appeal of its model as a way of constraint.

But there is another approach to overall capacity constraints—the one used in Germany, where the unusual mix of private implementation of public policy (see Chapter 5) is very pronounced in cost containment. By laws enacted in the late 1980s, Germany has set a firm policy that the worker-employer premiums must not increase faster than the rate of increase in worker incomes, which is an indirect way of stating that health care's priority as a share of GNP should remain stable. National wage and salary income thus becomes a global cap on health care revenues, which then translates into an expenditure cap as the sickness-funds managers negotiate annual provider payment rates. Because it is also national law that benefits should not be significantly curtailed, a financial balancing act is created whose burden falls largely on providers. Copayments (small ones) are not expected to play a major cost-control role there; rather, they are a way of paying for some expansion of the system without violating the premium limits.

An annual "summit" meeting of providers and sickness-funds officials called the Concerted Action Conference for Health results in recommendations for a nationwide level of increases in provider compensation, and these recommendations then become financial parameters for the funds' negotiations with hospitals and physicians. The bargaining with regional physician associations results in both a conversion factor for individual services in the fee schedule and a global budget for overall physician payments. The associations then become responsible both for payments to individual physicians on a fee-for-service basis and for adjusting the conversion figure downward if the sum of payments exceeds its quarterly share of the budget. With each hospital, a global budget is negotiated.

This complicated multipartied arrangement works: Health care costs in West Germany for 1990 were $1,287 per capita and a bit over 8 percent of GDP; the rate of change in health care costs for 1989 was a *negative* 1.8 percent.

From the viewpoint of ideas we might adopt, the great advantage of the German mode over the Canadian is that it uses national political authority to define a financial constraint on all parties in the system but decentralizes implementation to more than 1,000 nongovernmental payers and a score of private physician groups. The existence of our 1,500 insurers would not have to be challenged politically, nor would all payment decisions be centralized in Washington under this kind of plan.

But is the corporatist approach of private groups exercising what is essentially governmental authority over providers one that would fit our political-economic culture? I think not. Indeed, the mind boggles at the thought of the American Medical Association, or its state chapters, being given this kind of paymaster authority or accepting this kind of regulatory role over its members! However, new physician organizations might be developed in which membership is compulsory in order to legitimate bargaining on behalf of all physicians. From the start, the orientation of such new organizations might reduce the traditional predominance of economic self-protection found in the thinking of medical associations. As in Germany, there might be two sets of physician organizations; one would be the doctors' lobbying arm and the other would play a publicly responsible role.

The new Medicare fee schedule with soft volume controls shows that we can learn some explicit lessons from other systems, and Medicare does seem to be moving in a direction that will require some kind of physician-government bargaining, even if new institutions have to be developed. In fact, we may have the beginnings of a government-provider cooperative system in two very influential advisory bodies established in the 1980s.

These are the Prospective Payment Assessment Commission (ProPAC), started with the adoption of the DRG system, and the Physician Payment Review Commission (PPRC), which did much to gain the acceptance of the resource-based relative value scale. Both were congressionally established to monitor and fine-tune these innovative and politically risky ventures into medical price controls. With membership structured to include representatives of major viewpoints and interests, these organizations act as buffers between the government and the provider communities, juggling efforts to achieve a more effective health care system with helping Congress devise ways to squeeze costs in Medicare (and, to a lesser extent, in Medicaid). They operate through staff studies and public hearings in which testimony is heard from interest groups and independent analysts, and they feed information and recommendations to appropriate congressional committees as well as to HCFA through both annual reports and presentations to congressional committees.

ProPAC and PPRC have carved for themselves an unusual niche in American policymaking. With their great credibility in Washington, they may constitute the nucleus of a unique negotiating structure that could develop agreement among government, providers, business payers, insurers, and patient-oriented groups on an overall design for cost containment. Although the cooperative group-government relationships normal to Germany are almost a polar opposite to the adversarial U.S. business-government relationship, perhaps the professional ethos is still sufficiently strong to support public-interest-oriented institutions. That may be a naive hope, but the vise of payer demand for cost controls and provider insistence on avoiding a centralized public health care delivery system may yet provide the squeeze needed to impel us into a new age.

Pros and Cons of Global Budgeting

If global budgeting and overall capacity constraints can be devised, we would unquestionably have a stronger handle on costs. That is purpose number one; but there would be other pluses, too. GB has two strong medical advantages over existing approaches to cost control. Clinical autonomy, enjoyed by doctors in Germany, Canada, and Britain far more than here, is the first. In Germany, for example, the doctors' own associations perform utilization review, using physician profiling as the crucial tool. Combining this with their payment method allows the doctors to decide for themselves on the balance between economic and clinical autonomy. In Canada, there has been even less oversight (though that is changing). In other words, global expenditure caps reduce the need for micromanagement. PPRC has suggested that if Medicare's volume performance standards achieve their cost-control objectives, physicians here might be permitted more discretion regarding review activities. That would surely be a major plus for U.S. physicians, who have been called "the most litigated-against, second-guessed, and paperwork-laden physicians in western industrialised democracies."[5]

A second advantage is that global budgets enable policymakers to establish priorities within the activities or institutions encompassed in the expenditure cap, for example, making an explicit trade-off to ensure primary care for all by establishing waiting lists for elective surgeries. There's a lot to be said for any organizational pattern that encourages explicit consideration of priorities, because *no* system is going to have the resources with which to fulfill all demands put upon it.

Once the pattern of resources has been established and a financial cap set, then the individual physician's opportunity and responsibility is to work out a practice mode that maximizes appropriate services to her patients while adapting to the policy-determined limits.

One argument against global budgeting appeals to many physician groups and other providers: Overall limits may be achievable only by placing a lid on charges for services. From a public policy perspective, that is indeed part of the point. Some fees are excessive (and the RVS is a response within Medicare), and more are earned by performing unnecessary services. Global budgeting is intended to stimulate efforts toward more efficient and better-targeted services, which is where the outcomes and guidelines research comes in.

From a patient perspective, there is the objection that a resource cap will lead to rationing of care that will leave some needs unmet. The queuing in Britain and Canada is, it is true, in part a consequence of global budgeting; but queuing also reflects a set of priorities that emphasizes basic care for all over elective surgery for a few.

If GB should take the form of limiting health care expenditure increases to the rate of increase in GDP, there would indeed be a question of perhaps having to sacrifice too much in quality of care, so long as the health care inflation rate is so much higher than the overall CPI rate of increase. But because the whole point is to squeeze down medical inflation, the answer would not be to abandon the global budgeting concept but to use gradual phasing to ease the adjustment pattern. Perhaps if we had overall GB as part of a national plan, the allowed health care increase might be set at GDP growth plus, say, 4 percent the first two years, then 2 percent, then at the same level as GDP. By that time, it is hoped, hospitals would have learned how to run tighter ships, regionalization could take hold, and physicians might be following a more conservative mode of practice and using guidelines for some of the more expensive procedures.

There is a con side to GB, but it is part of the necessary price to be paid if universal access must be accompanied, for political reasons, by effective cost control.

Can global budgeting be done in this country? Yes. It is being done every day by physicians in HMOs, in hospitals whose equip-

ment may not all be state-of-the-art, and in working with patients
lacking adequate coverage.

Global budgeting for our entire system is probably a long way off,
but we may achieve cost gains by developing areas of partial GB, and
HMOs are an example. A staff- or group-model HMO with physicians
on salary and owning its own facilities *is* global budgeting for its
subscribers. Per capita monthly-yearly premiums multiplied by the
number of members equals an institutional budget. If we assume (as
we must) professional integrity and an absence of insidious financial
incentives to increase a doctor's income by using fewer resources on
his patients, then an HMO with a broad range of specialties is a
small-scale model of global budgeting. And the record of such organizations shows that a primary way of saving money is their physicians' adoption of a practice style that emphasizes prevention and
ambulatory care. This fits Wennberg's observation that "clinical
algorithms adapt to available resources in remarkable ways."[6]

At a much lower level, DRGs are a form of partial global budgeting
because they replace reimbursement for a sum of individual charges
made by a hospital with a single amount for a given procedure. Per
diem rates for hospitalization are another. Under discussion among
Medicare policymakers and private insurers is the idea of bundling
the doctor's fee with related personnel costs (anesthesiologist, assist-
ing physician, operating-room technician, pre- and postop visits,
etc.) into a single medical fee, also prospective.

A capacity restraint on a specific type of resource can also be an
effective way to avoid unnecessary, even wasteful, expenditures. In
the late 1970s, attempts were made to use Certificate-of-Need (CON)
programs to slow down the proliferation of hospital beds and expensive equipment. Provider domination of the reviewing bodies often
(but not always) negated such efforts, and the deregulation fervor of
the early Reagan years led to its dismantling. However, the post-CON
competitive frenzy in hospital building, in establishing transplant
facilities and teams, and in spreading MRIs strongly suggests that a
more sophisticated try at regional facilities planning might have a
substantial payoff.

Intensive care units (ICUs) may provide an example. They account for 10 percent of all medical costs, yet researchers have
estimated that 30 percent of patients in ICUs are not sick enough to
need them and 10 percent are too sick to benefit. Regional planning
might bring need and supply into better balance; in its absence a

kind of Parkinson's law apparently applies: If the ICU bed is there, it will be used.

A much more controversial capacity control would limit medical-school admissions. Ironically, in light of our failure to treat everyone needing care, we already have one of the highest physician-to-population ratios. And it continues to increase—153 doctors per 1,000 people in 1970, 192 in 1980, and 220 estimated for 1990. Because it is the doctor who determines 70 percent of the system's expenditures by ordering tests and deciding on hospitalization, the argument is made that fewer doctors per 1,000 patients would mean lower system costs overall. Because the experts disagree on whether a shortage or a surplus of physicians is more likely 10 years from now, this control is not one to be lightly imposed. (And never as an edict; the most likely control would be a reduction of governmental support for medical education, which would then lead the schools themselves to reduce supply.)

There are, as the old saying goes, many ways to skin a cat. And if our pluralist, provider-oriented health care politics makes national global budgeting a far-off goal, policymaker ingenuity and fluid politics under pressure from payers may nevertheless enable us to make meaningful advances in cost containment along the lines begun with DRGs, the relative value scale and volume performance standards, practice guidelines, technology assessments, and the stronger forms of HMOs.

Rationing: The Ultimate Cost Control?

In 1984 an economist-physician team of health care writers, Henry J. Aaron and Dr. William B. Schwartz, published a book about thinking the unthinkable in cost control. In *The Painful Prescription: Rationing Hospital Care*, they argued that the only way to avoid having increasing health expenditures yield benefits not worth their costs would be to ration (defined as denying beneficial care).

Then leading bioethicist Daniel Callahan, in *Setting Limits: Medical Goals in an Aging Society*, carried the argument into more controversial territory by advocating that the aged be singled out for such rationing. To allow more budgetary room for meeting health needs of the nonelderly, and nonhealth needs generally, Callahan said that after one had lived a "natural life span" (i.e., age late 70s or early 80s), the treatment question should become not whether a beneficial technology existed but whether there was any obligation to use it.

Although his proposals have received much more media attention than policymaker endorsement, his writings have probably helped to undergird the spread of voluntary self-rationing in the form of living wills and durable powers of attorney.

Rationing is now widely discussed but perhaps not clearly defined. It would be shamefully premature to move at this time toward rationing as generally understood.

Dictionaries define rationing not simply as denying something—which would reasonably make it a fearful term in health care discussions—but as distributing equally or equitably some commodity or resource in scarce supply. The term has an ethical component; it is not just a matter of value-free economics.

The linkage of rationing with equity is clear if we think of the nation's World War II experience. Rationing—generally by coupon books that took into account size of family, or travel necessity in the case of gasoline—was a response to physical shortages of sugar, meat, gasoline, and other essential commodities. Distributing these according to ability to pay would have violated our sense of social ethics, for millions of people would have been completely deprived.

At least for those of us old enough to recall World War II, that's what rationing is about:

- A response to a shortage of real resources, not just of money
- A distribution problem that the price system cannot equitably solve
- A determination of equitable distribution on the basis of comparative need for the particular scarce resource
- A deliberate policy choice made by accountable representatives of the community-at-large for reasons of the public interest—not just a financial strategy of payers

Does the current health care situation fit these criteria for rationing? Hardly. Hospital beds have been in excess supply, in the aggregate, for years, and ever more so as care moves to ambulatory settings. A physician surplus is widely forecast (although that is disputed), and in most urban areas there is certainly no overall shortage. These being the two most vital resources to be distributed, there is simply no case to be made for rationing as a response to a physical resource shortage.

Only if we say that there is a real shortage of money with which to pay for health care can we defend true rationing today. But how could the United States, with a GNP of $5 trillion and still one of the highest per capita incomes in the world, assert that it cannot afford to provide health care for all of its citizens when countries with far lower income statistics manage to do it? And how could Medicare justify squeezing its beneficiaries with rationing when its own administrative house is in such bad order that its financial intermediaries are sometimes paying providers $400 for a $70 TENS unit (a pain-relieving machine)?

Does all this mean that it is wrong, or at least a waste of time, to discuss rationing? No, for at least two reasons. First, we *are* rationing in the simpler, half-true sense that not everyone gets all available beneficial care. State Medicaid programs are, unfortunately, excellent examples of denial-of-care rationing, by people categories rather than by services. So are the increasing insurance company denials of coverage. Overall, recall, we distribute health services in the United States on a market basis. Without money or insurance, one is denied care. Not an acceptable form of rationing in our scheme of rhetorical values, even though we don't practice what we preach about a right to health care. Open discussion of the kind of rationing we now have may help shame us into doing something better.

For example, recognizing both the inequity and ineffectiveness of current limitations on who gets care from Medicaid, Oregon is, as I write, seeking a federal OK to experiment with a Medicaid plan that would include *everyone* with below-poverty income; the trade-off is that some *services* would be excluded from coverage. A priority list based on a combination of cost-effectiveness analysis and public reactions is to be used to refuse services falling below the point at which the anticipated aggregate cost of services equals the annual appropriation by the state legislature. This would be a kind of global budget for the poor, with a much more rational (in terms of cost-effectiveness) use of funds than often occurs today. However, although the Oregon plan would enable all of the poor to get some services, the denial of some services would apply only to pregnant women, mothers, and children, not to the elderly, blind, and disabled on whom 70 percent of the Medicaid budget is spent. So that plan still fails the equity test in the definition of rationing. True rationing with explicit limits on the amount of care can only be fair when done under a universal system in which *all* citizens face the same limits. When all is said and done, Oregon's contribution may be limited to having highlighted the appalling inadequacies of the existing Medicaid hodgepodge.

Second, if we were to adopt some form of global budgeting, a context would then exist in which a more legitimate form of rationing could be used. Because GB would bring with it capacity constraints on facilities and on big-ticket diagnostic equipment and treatment methods, American physicians would, as noted earlier, have to adjust their treatment criteria to available resources, and that means implicit rationing: comparing the relative needs of all patients who could use a particular scarce resource. Waiting lists would be the concrete expression of the patient priorities thus established. (And if you react to the notion of queuing with horror as something un-American, please remember that millions of our low-income patients wait weeks and months even for ordinary treatment such as prenatal care, and that 36 million Americans do not even have a right to get in a line!) Policymakers for the community, not the individual physician, would properly bear the responsibility of determining priorities in the overall provision of resources.

Will we be able to avoid more explicit forms of rationing? One way would be to do well with all the other forms of cost control discussed earlier. But perhaps even all of those will be insufficient unless we change the culture of medicine to the less aggressive style of other nations, and the expectations of patients away from the irresponsible individualism that physicians have often encouraged (at least with their well-insured patients). With those changes, we could almost certainly save billions of dollars by changing the criterion of utilization (at least for the more expensive items) from Is it possibly beneficial? to Is it of proven effectiveness? It would take a very sanguine perception of our capacity for rational social change to expect that such transformations will soon be forthcoming.

Another way to avoid rationing would be to let the share of national product used in health care continue—by default—to escalate faster than most other areas of production.

Far better, however, would be a much faster growth rate in GNP than we have obtained in recent years. That might well be the best thing the national government could use its policy tools to encourage, for it would allow health care expenses (and those of other needed programs, too) to increase without adding to health care's share of national income. This would not be cost control as such, but share-of-resources control, which matters more.

prenatal care, and that 36 million Americans do not even have a right to get in a line!) Policymakers for the community, not the individual physician, would properly bear the responsibility of determining priorities in the overall provision of resources.

Will we be able to avoid more explicit forms of rationing? One way would be to do well with all the other forms of cost control discussed earlier. But perhaps even all of those will be insufficient unless we change the culture of medicine to the less aggressive style of other nations, and the expectations of patients away from the irresponsible individualism that physicians have often encouraged (at least with their well-insured patients). With those changes, we could almost certainly save billions of dollars by changing the criterion of utilization (at least for the more expensive items) from Is it possibly beneficial? to Is it of proven effectiveness? It would take a very sanguine perception of our capacity for rational social change to expect that such transformations will soon be forthcoming.

Another way to avoid rationing would be to let the share of national product used in health care continue—by default—to escalate faster than most other areas of production.

Far better, however, would be a much faster growth rate in GNP than we have obtained in recent years. That might well be the best thing the national government could use its policy tools to encourage, for it would allow health care expenses (and those of other needed programs, too) to increase without adding to health care's share of national income. This would not be cost control as such, but share-of-resources control, which matters more.

The assessment of longtime economist–health policy analyst Eli Ginzberg is probably as realistic as any of the estimates circulating today:

> A society such as ours—which places a high value on pluralism, which is enthralled by technology, which resists domination by the federal government, which accepts the prevailing inequality of income and wealth, and which promotes the sovereignty of consumers—is not likely to opt for serious constraints on biomedical research and development or to favor the explicit rationing of proved health care services to the public. Its concerns are more likely to be focused on ensuring access for the entire population to an effective level of care and on finding a way of covering the health care costs of those who cannot pay their own way. Until we approach the upper limit of acceptable health care expenditures—an eventuality that may be far in the future—cost containment is likely to remain the elusive hare that the hounds pursue but never overtake.[7]

Part Four

Components of an Achievable Better System

8
Elements for an Optimal Health Care Plan

Instead of offering one more plan, I will sketch the building blocks that should be included in an optimal plan—blocks whose particular combination will necessarily be shaped by the compromises of the legislative process, not by analysts' blueprints.

By *optimal* I do not mean *ideal*. It is time to recognize that reformers' ideal plans can be the enemy of good though imperfect reforms. An optimal plan will be one that can be passed within the substantial constraints imposed by the concatenation of our pluralistic political culture, private enterprise economic ideology, business and employment interests vested in the status quo, federal-state buck-passing competition, and the paralyzing combination of antitax sentiment and federal budget deficits.

Within that framework, the questions to focus on are these:

- What features of a delivery system—organizationally, financially, governmentally, substantively—will best achieve universal access to needed care?

- What forms of cost containment are most likely to be effective, consistent with maximum coverage and high quality, and not access-limiting on the basis of one's economic position?

The Givens of Reform

Every actor in the system—patient, doctor, hospital, nurse, payer, insurance company, state governments, federal government, even manufacturers and suppliers of drugs and devices—has a proposal to offer, but the second-best for each of them seems to be no change at all. Legislatures sometimes act despite objections from a strong lobby; but Congress and state legislatures are unlikely to enact major changes if the interests with large economic stakes form a solid

How Much Change Is the Public Ready For?

Proponents of universal health insurance, especially of the Canadian variety, like to seize upon selective results of public opinion polls to bolster their political case. Among the most cited is a 1988 poll by Louis Harris and Associates in which 89 percent responded that our system needs fundamental change (despite majorities expressing satisfaction with their most recent doctor and hospital visits). Furthermore, 61 percent preferred the Canadian system when described as one in which government uses taxes to pay for health care for everyone, with free choice of physician.

Sounds great—until we look further. A 1990 Roper poll found that among those preferring the Canadian system only 57 percent retained that view when asked about paying substantially greater taxes to support it, and three other recent polls found that the higher the taxes needed for a better system, the lower the public support, in direct proportion. As more detailed information and options reach the public, opinions become more finely differentiated. In 1991 during the Thornberg-Wofford Senate race, a poll found that 35 percent of people asked preferred an all-government plan and 32 percent preferred a plan in which employers had to provide coverage or else pay taxes for a public plan.

It is not really surprising that what starts as strong support for a policy innovation often evaporates as the specific costs (in various senses) are brought to people's attention. This happens all the time. Polls on environmental protection show exactly the same phenomenon: Eighty-five percent often respond to a poll with enthusiasm for strong protection against air or water pollution; then many of the same persons object when it turns out that jobs created by economic development would be lost or not created if those protective measures were implemented.

phalanx in opposition and if that opposition strikes a responsive chord in general public opinion.

The first assumption of any proposal with a hope of enactment is therefore that compromise will be a basic element. Critics will charge that "lowest common denominator" politics have been at work—and that will probably be true to some extent. That's how things work, with only rare exceptions. Our failure over twenty years to achieve consensus on any one reform proposal should ring alarm bells in our heads. There are so many competing schemes not because of scientific uncertainty but because of great differences in priorities that have to be factored into any reform, and in the proposer's degree of political optimism or pessimism, flexibility or rigidity about what is acceptable.

Ambivalence abounds in public opinion, often as a result of ignorance, the extent of which should not be minimized. Consider the 1988
Catastrophic Coverage amendments to Medicare. A survey of the elderly done in the midst of debate over repeal revealed an astounding
lack of accurate information in the minds of intended beneficiaries. The
major new coverage, for example, would have been for prescription
drugs, yet almost two-thirds were unaware of this. Much discussed in
the press was the fact that the law would *not* cover extended nursing-home time, yet over 80 percent thought it would cover six months.
And only 9 percent correctly responded to a true-false assertion that all
of the elderly would have to pay more in taxes to cover the new
benefits. This last is, I think, significant in showing that when there is a
lot of furor—and among the wealthier who would in fact have paid
significantly more, there was what the press calls a fire storm—people
react emotionally on a worst-case expectation basis. If Medicare beneficiaries can be so confused about legislation designed specifically for
them, one cannot make even a rational guess how things may turn out
when the political public relations machinery is cranked up by competing interests over national health insurance legislation.

The only apparent consensus so far is the two-sided one that something should be done to bring down costs and ensure coverage but
that whatever is done should not disrupt our satisfactory relationships
with our own doctors and hospitals and should not involve substantial
additional taxation.

The volatility and contradictory qualities of public opinion do not
mean that nothing can be done. But on the basis of the polling data
now available one has to be very pessimistic about the chances of
support for a wholesale change to an entirely tax-supported health care
system that would displace the existing pluralistic arrangements.

Political prediction being far more art than science, and political
scientists being analysts, not politicians, I do not pretend to be able
to provide fine-tuned estimates—or even guestimates—of what will
emerge whenever we finally act. But some boundaries are clear
enough to state with little hesitation.

The first and firmest limiting fact is that the country is far from
ready to enact a single, government-directed, national health insurance plan—one that would be totally tax-financed, eliminating both
employer sponsorship and private insurance. The ideological, political, and budgetary obstacles are just too great, barring an unlikely
political miracle.

But, advocates may protest, isn't that too pessimistic in light of
public opinion polls showing high percentages calling for substantial

changes in the system? No, because those polling results are in good part an artifact of the wording of the questions and the context in which they are asked, and of respondent ignorance of both the tax-cost implications and the disruptions of existing relationships involved.

Full-scale adoption of the Canadian plan is not in the cards, in my judgment, nor is its most widely advocated professionally sponsored equivalent, the one espoused by Physicians for a National Health Plan.

Almost equally beyond the pale, from a quite different perspective, is the competitive HMO model advocated most forcefully by Enthoven. Its basic problems are the impracticality of organizing an all-pervasive network of multiple HMOs and public sponsors for them, plus the corollary difficulties of persuading the bulk of the population to give up free choice of physician, and physicians to give up fee-for-service practice. A more likely estimate of HMOs' place in the system is that their growth will continue in the almost flat trajectory of the past couple of years, and that would not augur well for Enthoven's plan.

Another political given is that no legislation will pass that does not include some real cost controls. This argues against both the AMA's Health Access America and the Senate Democratic leadership's 1991 version of the Rockefeller-Pepper Report plan.

It may be that we do not have the discipline to practice as strong a form of resource constraints as used by other nations with parliamentary political systems less subject to immediate tides of public opinion. The debacle of Congress hastily repealing in 1989 catastrophic Medicare coverage it had enacted with much fanfare in 1988 is a good case in point. Still, we won't know what we can do unless we try, and the strident cries of institutional payers may just provide the backbone needed to rein in the not-very-cost-conscious habits of the providers. There might even be some popular appeal—which would increase as the cost-sharing burden of employer cost-shifting onto employees rises—for a financing system that limits health care spending increases to the rate of increase in national product or to wage gains. People would like the limits and might accept the implicit rationing entailed in the facilities and equipment constraints (if they were not very severe) necessarily created by such budget limits.

I do want to set a basic limit on how far we should go with cost control—one that arises from personal values, not from political expectations. In my value system (and I suspect a majority of the citizenry would agree), ensuring coverage for all Americans is the first priority, and cost control is the second. We need to combine both, but if cost controls lead to arbitrary reductions in care in individual cases for economic reasons, then cost control should be eased before care is denied. This may or may not be politically realistic, but it is ethically correct for a society that believes health care is a right.

So, what would be the elements of an optimal plan within these boundaries?

Elements of an Optimal Plan

Play-or-Pay: A Middle Way

To ensure access to health care through universal insurance coverage, the play-or-pay (PoP) option is best.

- Unlike a universal public plan, Canadian style, PoP does not require dismantling the existing system of multiple payers, the private insurance industry, employer sponsorship, and supplementary public programs.

- Like the quasipublic German plan, PoP could retain institutional pluralism while putting the authority of the national government behind some firm regulatory controls.

- Unlike the earlier employer-mandate plans, its two-track feature could be a part of financing coverage for everyone, not just employees.

- Unlike further expansion of Medicaid, PoP reaches the 75 percent of the uninsured who are employed.

- A fixed tax rate for the pay option would give much-sought stability and predictability to business in handling its health care costs.

- Because PoP would establish a precedent for using employer-employee contributions in a publicly defined system, its public program could eventually become the base on which a true

universal public system could be developed—if and when a
political window of opportunity opened at a later time.

Late in 1991 there was a sign that play-or-pay might have the
beginnings of an effective coalition. The National Leadership Coalition for Health Care Reform, with ex-presidents Gerald R. Ford and
Jimmy Carter as honorary cochairs, announced a play-or-pay plan
that would include setting an annual national expenditure target
and uniform reimbursement rates for all providers in all plans.
Although some firms active earlier disengaged themselves from the
mandatory aspects of the plan, some stayed with it, including Beth-
lehem Steel, Safeway, Time Warner, American Nurses Association,
U.S. Bancorps, Chrysler, Xerox Corporation, Southern California
Edison, and Dayton-Hudson. This is the broadest coalition yet to
endorse a particular approach. Still, one's optimism has to be re-
strained, for some corporations with low wages and high worker
turnover rates, such as Marriott, Kmart, and Burger King belong to
the Partnership on Health Care and Employment, formed to lobby
against any mandatory approach. In short, there is some movement
toward agreement but a long way to go.

Public Financing's Role

Because total insurance costs will increase as the previously uninsured are covered, the employer-employee premium costs under
play-or-pay will have to be supplemented with government revenues. These should be partly federal, partly state, giving both levels
of government a share in the pain and an incentive to spend the
money carefully. The states should be free to tap whatever revenue
sources they find feasible; the national revenues could come from a
sales or payroll tax. (I would personally prefer that *all* programs be
paid out of a progressive income tax, but to recommend that would
really be to tilt at windmills. Polls show a general public preference
for taxes other than income taxes.)

Should the existing tax subsidy for employer-sponsored coverage
be eliminated? No. Elimination is argued for because it inequitably
gives a subsidy to employed persons, but not to the unemployed
(who may need it more), and because the higher one's tax bracket,
the greater the subsidy. But elimination of the tax subsidy would
lead to a greater inequity. Without the subsidy, many employers

would drop insurance entirely, and the low-paid would be hurt the worst. Also, health coverage is part of the bargained compensation in many large firms, yet its cash equivalent in take-home pay would most likely not immediately replace it.

Universalism

There's an old, true saying that "a program for the poor is a poor program." Just compare Medicare and Medicaid. The latter identifies the patient as a nonworking welfare client. The former awards coverage regardless of economic or social standing. Medicare's coverage criteria thus both protect the dignity of the patient and ensure tremendous political support for the program, because Medicare coverage applies to *us*, not just to *them*.

Here we should draw on Canadian experience. Perhaps the best thing about their system, beyond covering everyone, is that wealthy, poor, and middle-income patients all present the same card to providers and must be treated equally. When there are waiting lists, the priority is by need, not by personal income or happenstance of employer coverage. In the United States, the public program supported (at least in part) by the pay alternative assessments on employers should replace Medicaid and be open on a sliding-scale basis to those not far above the poverty line who are outside the work force or in the very smallest firms if political compromise dictates that they be exempt from play-or-pay. Means testing would then be based on the goal of including everyone in a broad program rather than excluding the better-off from a program for the poor. Eligibility cards can be identical for all enrollees regardless of who the payer is, thus helping to ensure single-tier treatment of all enrollees, which is a prime goal of universalism.

Cost-sharing Without Harming Access

It is reasonable that we all share in paying for health care. But, as I argued earlier, instead of making copayments at the time of needing treatment, employees should share costs by paying a portion of the insurance cost through payroll deduction. Cost-sharing at the time of treatment should be limited to token payments of a very few dollars—perhaps payable by those of poverty income with chits provided by the public program office. Minimal payments at time of treatment would perhaps serve as a useful stop-and-think safeguard against frivolous use of care, and they would have a positive effect by making self-responsibility an explicit value.

Avoiding Free Riders

A small portion of the medically uninsured are people who could afford (as much as many others, anyway) to share in the costs of 80–20 employer-offered insurance but choose not to, taking their chances on sickness or accidents. It is both irritating and unfair that emergency care costs for this minority contribute to everyone else's insurance and tax costs. When a universal system is offered, signing up should be compulsory for all members of the work force, including the wealthiest executives and the lowest-paid hourly wage workers. That's fairness as I think most of us understand it. And it will help to spread the total costs on a "community rating" basis, an aspect of a universal approach that makes health coverage, at least in part, a social insurance kind of program, like Social Security.

Scope of Coverage

From a wishful-thinking perspective, a health care program intended to assure access should include all services that might be beneficial, from prenatal and preventive to acute and chronic, and should include those requiring long-term care in nursing homes. In the real world, agreeing on a plan for acute care and some basic and clearly cost-effective prevention measures might be as much as we could initially handle. Long-term care financing presents so many additional complexities that its inclusion in an initial package would be more likely to sink the whole effort than to extend the coverage. Until acute care is taken care of, Medicaid's de facto place as the public program for nursing-home needs should continue.

The acute care plan should include all medically necessary hospital and physician services. Beyond that, and admitting that "necessary" is hard to define, inclusion of prescription drugs, rehabilitative services, and behavioral health care may be dependent on the detailed financial estimates of cost and political estimates of bearable revenue burdens that can only be made as very concrete elements are put together during the legislative process. It may be necessary to violate the earlier recommendation against copayments in order to include these at all. But partial coverage would be better than none.

We need to remember that Medicare and middle-class employer-sponsored health plans also have limits. Some policies exclude prenatal and birthing care; few cover periodic mammography screening; many (including Medicare) exclude or limit prescription drugs and behavioral medicine; most exclude such medical devices as hearing aids and eyeglasses. The goal is to offer access to mainstream medical care regardless of income, but we cannot insist that publicly supported programs all be equal to the very best of private plans paid for with the highest premiums—at least until (a long way off) we insist that universal public education means equality in facilities and services among all school districts and between public and private schools.

What Roles for the States?

Not many years ago, many (myself included) would have given the states a very small role. Their administrative capacities were often rudimentary, with spoils systems still in operation for selection of public personnel. The federal government was perceived as both more sympathetic to social benefit programs and more capable of financing them and running them effectively. Today the national government is in a fiscal morass while the states have become administratively stronger—though also in bad financial condition until a strong recovery occurs.

We must give the states a substantial role, both financial and operational. Cooperative federalism, in which grants from Washington are supplemented with state monies and the states run a program within broad federal guidelines, has become the normal mode of operation for many domestic programs since the early 1960s. Clean air and water programs, for example, set national effluent standards and then call upon the states to establish implementation plans.

The public program that would cover both workers involved in the "pay" part of play-or-pay and those who have been Medicaid enrollees should be run by the states, as Medicaid is now. But the states would no longer be allowed to cut off eligibility at very low income levels as a way of saving money. Also, services available to clients must not be differentiated by how clients get into the program (except for Medicare rules on its beneficiaries who are also in Medicaid).

States would be allowed program choices, for example, they could buy optional coverages, coverage for beneficiaries in private PPOs and capitated HMOs, or extra prevention services and could use insurance companies as intermediaries or to establish public offices for operations, fee schedules, and DRGs. Experimentation with alternative approaches to delivering health services could be one of the truly major contributions of the states. Combining state and local public health department services with public insurance clinics like community health centers, tying preventive health programs into public-school operations, and pioneering broader use of physician assistants and nurse practitioners to strengthen rural health care accessibility are among the thrusts that might be developed aggressively. Some states might thus develop successful programs that could serve as models to improve both access and cost control nationwide. On the financial side, too, the responsibilities of the states would be extensive and would include both providing revenue and—at least as crucial in shaping the health care system—setting the upward limits of public expenditures.

Constraining Budgets, Controlling Costs

We need not move to an all-public-sector system to use the global budgeting form of cost containment that is generally thought to be a major factor in Canada's lower per capita costs. Because we also have a federal form of government, our national government's grants to the states for its portion of the universal coverage plan could be capped according to a policy that the grants' year-by-year growth not exceed the rate of growth in national income or gross national product, or (to follow the German example) the rate of increase in average wage and salary income. The states would then be in the hot seat, responsible for providing health care services that met a federal standard but (as in Canada) not able to count on open-ended federal matching funds to bear all possible cost escalation. Only by vigorous and effective cost containment could the states meld the service and financial dimensions within their individual political tax capacity limits. Setting hospital global budgets and controlling physician fees and the volume of services (perhaps adopting and adapting Medicare's formulas) are probable tools. Resources would thus be constrained at both national and state levels, providing powerful stimuli for all the partial cost controls described in Chapter 6. Practitioners would be inevitably encouraged to rethink their cultural practice styles and pay close attention to cost-effectiveness of alternative modes of treatment.

Why argue for resource limits in a supposedly optimal health coverage plan? Why not just argue for open-ended health care financing? After all, there is nothing sacrosanct about 12 percent of GNP as a limit. Resource limits are necessary, however, because the competition for social services resources is intense. Our goal is universal good health, and it is likely that we could prevent many health problems by investing more in education, food and nutrition, housing for the homeless, job training, and other social services.

As indicated at the end of Chapter 7, I believe that if rigid cost controls reached the point of reducing care in ways that led to public revolt, then our political system would respond by lifting the limits, softening the controls. But if we do not make our best-faith effort, we will surely be wasting resources that will go to increase provider incomes without delivering cost-effective, useful care.

Encourage Professionalism, Discourage Micromanagement

Last but very definitely not least of the elements desirable in health care reform plans is that emphasis in treatment choices should be on providing incentives for health care professionals to be just that: professionals, not mere "providers" like manufacturers of automobiles or purveyors of rental videos. Professionalism is an honorable concept of great historical lineage. It carries with it an obligation to put the public good ahead of maximizing private gain in return for a high degree of autonomy of operation on the basis of special skills and knowledge. Perhaps the greatest error of recent years in the national government's health policy has been to treat medicine like a competitive business in which the bottom line is the primary guide to behavior. Professionalism cannot flourish in that atmosphere.

Physicians, and especially their self-appointed organized spokesgroups like the AMA, must blame themselves in good part because their failure to pay much attention to costs and their opposition to any controls at all helped create a mood (among legislators and private payers alike) for blunt-nosed financial controls. Also, because there was no overall strategy consistent with leaving more of the

---

Preserving Pluralism

Pluralism seems to be almost a dirty word sometimes—and for good reason if you want substantial changes in public policy. The check-and-balance, tug-and-haul, near paralysis of our separation-of-powers political institutions is maddening when a need is clear but the decision process is stalemated. A shift in the balance to make it a little bit easier for policy initiatives—including specifically a substantially changed health care system—to be enacted would make for a better constitutional system, in my view. But that is not about to happen. We will continue to work with what we have, with occasional periods of strong political leadership providing the centripetal political force needed to overcome the pluralist fetters long enough to get something important done.

Although we might want to reduce governmental pluralism, we should be leery of attacking pluralism in the society at large. The multiplicity of interest groups; the mixed economy of private, not-for-profit, and public-sector enterprises; the demographic diversity of America; and the multifaceted struggle over whose picture of reality and whose values will be embedded in public policy—these are the true guardians against the "tyranny of the majority," and in my view they make most of the formal checks and balances unnecessary. They are also the source of our real "comparative advantages" as a nation: organizational and technological innovation, flexibility, experimentation, openness to new ideas and new approaches to problems, and divergent responses to accommodate the differing value patterns among the 50 states.

---

medical decisionmaking to the physicians and other professionals, public policymakers were fearful of tackling anything more than economics-based tinkering around the fringes, which led to an emphasis on details. Adoption of macrobudgetary constraints and use of partial global budgeting wherever possible would go far to restore a policy context conducive to professional autonomy and professional responsibility. Better health care with clearer access at as reasonable a cost as burgeoning technologies permit could be the positive result.

Plan A, Plan B

Two imperatives should be uppermost in design of a program that would pull together all these elements:

- Everyone should have basic acute coverage.
- Providers should be presented with strong budgetary restraints

I take these as positive aspects of social pluralism—aspects worth preserving in health care (as elsewhere) even if there is less administrative efficiency than under a single centralized system. Even close observers and proponents of the Canadian model have noted that the United States is ahead in such organizational innovations as community health centers and HMOs and in development of practice guidelines. The ferment in approaches to utilization review, cost-control incentives, and alternative delivery service patterns is so strong, and the absence of any magic bullet so clear, that the advantages of having 50 states as experimental laboratories and many hundreds of insurers and corporate payers vying with one another to find the most cost-effective approaches to care are worth retaining as a positive good—not just as a regrettable political necessity.

Another value of pluralism not to be ignored is its yardstick role. In the 1930s, the Tennessee Valley Authority (TVA) was established partly as a yardstick against which to measure the efficiency and values of private electric power utilities. Having a mixed system (like play-or-pay) in health care could accomplish the same goal in reverse, with the continuation of a large private insurance role providing a benchmark for the public system, for one cannot argue today that public monopolies will be without fault.

Strong pluralism needs strong, publicly set boundaries and limits to channel the energy and vigor it develops. But public control may be better exercised by regulating a mixed health economy than by creating an entirely governmental one.

against proliferation of unnecessary facilities and services.

A play-or-pay plan with a budgetary limit tied to macroeconomic growth (e.g., the proposal by Holahan and associates described in Chapter 5) would best combine these essentials.

Some of the other desirable features would flow as by-products of such an approach, and some others would be subject to the compromises needed to reach legislative agreement and move us beyond the two-decade debate over health care delivery reform.

What if play-or-pay proves unattainable at this time because of its partial public-sector orientation?

Probably the first-line alternative would be an employer mandate without the "or pay" side—the kind advocated by President Nixon two decades ago. If applied to all employers regardless of size, and if all workers were required to sign up, it would solve a good part of the financial access problem. However, to make this alternative even remotely acceptable to small business, there would first have to be legislation requiring community rating (which is needed in any case) and open enrollment periods, and perhaps even then legislation recognizing a need for some public subsidy of the smallest firms. Allowing small firms to buy in to Medicaid for their lower-income employees would be a possible halfway provision of value. Public provision for those not employed and not presently eligible for Medicaid would still be a necessary supplement in order to achieve universal coverage.

Expansions of Medicaid for mothers and small children in recent years have made it an increasingly meaningful, though very imperfect, safety net. The 1990 law requiring that states gradually add to the Medicaid rolls all children under 18 in families with below-poverty incomes will close another part of the access gap. But that will still leave out all poor adults under 65 who do not have child dependents. Putting them into Medicaid and developing a subsidized sliding-scale buy-in for the near-poor that would encourage but not ensure coverage would be the minimal incremental steps needed to supplement mandated coverage of the employed.

However, these Medicaid extensions would do nothing to improve the entire system; they would not create any overall cost strategy; and they would only exacerbate the cost problem for public payers. It is unlikely that so much additional burden could be placed on the states without adopting cost controls that would be likely to emphasize patient copayments—thus effectively erasing much of what coverage extension was meant to achieve. In other words, such patching up without more basic change is not really likely to work.

Time for Action, Time for Leadership

Incrementalism is not enough. For too long we have patched up here and developed new cracks there, when a new structure was clearly needed. For too long we have talked about a right to health care as a basic value but have failed to implement it. With middle- and even upper-income people becoming subject to the vagaries of a health market oriented more to the interests of providers and private payers than to those of patients, a modicum of political leadership—especially presidential leadership—could well move us a giant step forward in the way we meet our health care needs.

Will a real political leader for universal health care please step forward?

Notes

Chapter 1

1. In his book review of Rosemary Stevens, *In Sickness and in Wealth, New York Times* Book Review Section, August 20, 1989.

2. James S. Todd, "It Is Time for Universal Access, Not Universal Insurance," *New England Journal of Medicine* v. 321 no. 1 (July 6, 1989): 46–47.

3. James Quackenbush, quoted in Leslie Berkman, "Hospital Hot Seats," *Los Angeles Times,* May 8, 1988.

Chapter 2

1. Lawrence D. Brown, "The Managerial Imperative and Organizational Innovation in Health Services," chapter 3 of Eli K. Ginzberg, ed., *The U.S. Health Care System: A Look to the 1990s* (Totowa, NJ: Rowman and Allenheld, 1985).

2. Thomas A. Preston, *The Clay Pedestal* (New York: Scribner's, 2d edition, 1986), p. 147.

3. Paul Starr, *The Social Transformation of American Medicine* (New York: Basic Books, 1982), pp. 349–350.

Chapter 3

1. It is a pleasure to note that in one of the political oddities of a cost-cutting period, Congress in the late 1980s began gradually to separate eligibility for Medicaid from AFDC for pregnant women and children and to create some national uniformity. As of this writing, children under 7 and pregnant women are eligible for Medicaid with family incomes up to 133 percent of the federal poverty level. And 1990 legislation—thanks to an amazing collaboration between the U.S. Chamber of Commerce, the Children's Defense Fund, and the AMA, among others, in a Children's Medicaid Coalition—requires the states to include all poor children through the age of 18 by the year 2001. Children are at last joining the elderly as an advantaged category in our crazy-quilt health delivery pattern.

2. Quoted in Philip J. Hilts, "U.S. Measles Epidemic Tied to Flawed System," *New York Times,* January 9, 1991.

Sources for box: Irene Wielawski, "Cutbacks Force Clinics to Turn Away Needy," *Los Angeles Times,* September 9, 1990; Nadine Brozan, "Close of

Clinics Rocks Poor Women," *New York Times,* March 25, 1991; Quentin Young quote from Don Terry, "As Medicaid Fees Push Doctors Out, Chicago Patients Find Fewer Choices," *New York Times,* April 12, 1991.

Chapter 5

1. For examples, I rely mostly on plans proposed in the pages of the *Journal of the American Medical Association* rather than on the plans put forward by political candidates, because the former are generally more detailed and I want to avoid labeling (positively or negatively) by mere name association. The range covered in this chapter is broader than that in the political emphases of 1992, and this should prove useful as the further shaping of the health care reform debate continues after the election year.

2. Reardon quoted in John F. Dolan, "Oh, Canada?" *AARP Bulletin* (March 1990): 16; Lowe quoted in Barry Brown, "How Canada's Health System Works," *Business and Health* (July 1989): 30.

3. Robert G. Evans, "'We'll Take Care of It for You': Health Care in the Canadian Community," *Daedalus* v. 117 no. 4 (Fall 1988): 155–189.

4. Kevin Grumbach, et al., "Liberal Benefits, Conservative Spending," *Journal of the American Medical Association* v. 265 no. 19 (May 15, 1991): 2549–2554. An earlier version was published as David U. Himmelstein, et al., "A National Health Program for the United States," *New England Journal of Medicine* v. 320 no. 2 (January 12, 1989): 102–108.

5. I provide details of various proposals to illustrate with some detail the range of ideas bubbling up. But we need to recognize that no proposal is ever legislated in the same form as it was originally proposed. That is why the overall thrust and strategy of each proposal is the thing to keep one's eye on.

6. E. Richard Brown, "Health USA: A National Program for the United States," *Journal of the American Medical Association* v. 267 no. 4 (January 22/29, 1992): 552–558.

7. John D. Rockefeller IV, "A Call for Action: The Pepper Commission's Blueprint for Health Care Reform," *Journal of the American Medical Association* v. 265 no. 19 (May 15, 1991): 2507–2510.

8. Alain C. Enthoven and Richard Kronick, "Universal Health Insurance Through Incentives Reform," *Journal of the American Medical Association* v. 265 no. 19 (May 15, 1991): 2532–2536. For a more detailed earlier exposition, see Enthoven and Kronick, "A Consumer-Choice Health Plan for the 1990s," *New England Journal of Medicine* v. 320 no. 1 (January 5, 1989): 29–37 and v. 320 no. 2 (January 12, 1989): 94–101.

9. John Holahan, Marilyn Moon, W. Pete Welch, and Stephen Zuckerman, "An American Approach to Health System Reform," *Journal of the American Medical Association* v. 265 no. 19 (May 15, 1991): 2537–2540. A more complete presentation is in *Balancing Access, Costs, and Politics: The American Context for Health System Reform,* by the same authors (Washington, DC: Urban Institute Report 91-6, Urban Institute Press/University Press of America, 1991).

10. James S. Todd, et al., "Health Access America—Strengthening the US Health Care System," *Journal of the American Medical Association* v. 265 no. 19 (May 15, 1991): 2503–2506.

11. American Medical Association, *Health Access America* (Chicago, 1990).

12. Carl J. Schramm, "Health Care Financing for All Americans," *Journal of the American Medical Association* v. 265 no. 24 (June 26, 1991): 3296–3299.

13. Stuart M. Butler, "A Tax Reform Strategy to Deal with the Uninsured," *Journal of the American Medical Association* v. 265 no. 19 (May 15, 1991): 2541–2544.

Chapter 6

1. Quoted in Dean C. Coddington, et al., *The Crisis in Health Care* (San Francisco: Jossey-Bass, 1990), p. 263.

2. David M. Eddy, "Variations in Physician Practice: The Role of Uncertainty," *Health Affairs* v. 3 no. 2 (Summer 1984): 74–89.

3. Quoted in Julie Kosterlitz, "Cookbook Medicine," *National Journal* (March 9, 1991): 574–577.

Chapter 7

1. "At Large with Dennis L. Breo: HHS Secretary Louis Sullivan Speaks Out for Improved Health," *Journal of the American Medical Association* v. 265 no. 19 (May 15, 1991): 2573–2576.

2. Lynn Payer, *Medicine & Culture* (New York: Henry Holt, 1988), pp. 107, 133.

3. Judith Wilson Ross, "Personal Choice and Public Rationing," a paper presented September 8, 1990, at a conference on Aging and the Elderly, sponsored by Loma Linda University's Center for Christian Bioethics, Loma Linda, CA.

4. Gina Kolata, "Parents of Tiny Infants Find Care Choices Are Not Theirs," *New York Times*, September 29, 1991. And see the companion pieces: Elisabeth Rosenthal, "As More Tiny Infants Live, Choices and Burden Grow," *New York Times*, September 29, 1991; and Jane E. Brody, "A Quality of Life Determined by a Baby's Size," *New York Times*, October 1, 1991.

5. Philip R. Lee and Lynn Etheredge, "Clinical Freedom: Two Lessons for the UK from US Experience with Privatisation of Health Care," *The Lancet* (February 4, 1989): 263–265.

6. John E. Wennberg, "On Patient Need, Equity, Supplier-induced Demand, and the Need to Assess the Outcome of Common Medical Practices," *Medical Care* v. 23 no. 5 (May 1985): 519.

7. Eli Ginzberg, "A Hard Look at Cost Containment," *New England Journal of Medicine* v. 316 no. 18 (April 30, 1987): 1151–1154.

Acronyms and Glossary

Administrative services only (ASO). Insurance company contract with employer to process claims for self-insured programs.

ADS. See Alternative delivery system.

Advance directives. Patient's instructions specifying level and kinds of treatment or naming the person who is to make those decisions should the patient become incapacitated.

AFDC. Aid to Families with Dependent Children

AHA. American Hospital Association

AHCPR. Agency for Health Care Policy and Research

AIDS. Acquired Immune System Deficiency Syndrome

Alternative delivery system (ADS). Nontraditional modes of organizing health care services.

AMA. American Medical Association

ASO. See Administrative services only.

Balance billing. Charges by the provider in excess of costs that are covered by the insurer.

BCBSA. Blue Cross and Blue Shield Association

Capitation (or per capita). Payment per person rather than per service.

CAT-scan. Computer Assisted Tomography

CEO. Chief Executive Officer

Certificate of Need (CON). Regulatory control over additions to institutional capacity.

CHAMPUS. Civilian Health and Medical Program of the Armed Forces

CHC. Community Health Center

COBRA. Consolidated Omnibus Budget Reconciliation Act. Act of Congress that permits ex-employees or their dependents to purchase health insurance from former employer at group rates for a limited period of time.

Coinsurance. Share of insurance premium paid by the employee in an employer-sponsored health insurance program.

CON. See Certificate of Need.

Copayment. Share of provider's charge paid by the patient.

Corporatism. A cooperative relationship between private economic groups and government in which each is dependent on, and has obligations to, the other.

Cost containment. Phrase commonly used as a shorthand reference to a multitude of diverse efforts by payers to reduce the rate of health care cost inflation.

Cost-sharing. Various costs paid out-of-pocket by the insured patient. See Deductibles, Copayments, Coinsurance.

Cost-shifting. Increasing charges to one payer to compensate for a provider's inability to collect full fees from another.

CPI. Consumer Price Index

Cross subsidy. Payment above cost by one party helps to pay for services to another paying less than full costs.

DCP. See Defined contribution plan.

Deductibles. Amount patient pays out-of-pocket each year before insurance benefits begin.

Defined contribution plan (DCP). Pension or health insurance plans in which employer guarantees to contribute a certain dollar level rather than any particular level of benefits.

Diagnostic Related Group (DRG). Prospective payment system in which a flat amount is paid to hospitals for each of about 480 treatments and procedures.

DRG. See Diagnostic Related Group.

Durable power of attorney for health care. Form of advance directive specifying a person to act as surrogate decisionmaker if patient is incapacitated.

Entitlement system. A program in which one is entitled to benefits by fitting into a statutory category and government is obligated to cover all entitled services, regardless of total cost.

EPO. See Exclusive Provider Organization.

Exclusive Provider Organization (EPO). Insurance arrangement in which the member patient must use a provider on the organization's list or else there is no coverage.

FASB. Federal Accounting Standards Board

FDA. Food and Drug Administration

Fee-for-Service (FFS). Traditional mode of payment in which payer is charged retrospectively for each specific service that has been performed.

FFS. See Fee-for-Service.

First-dollar coverage. Insurance in which there are no deductibles or other copayments.

GB. See Global budgeting.

GDP. See Gross Domestic Product.

Global budgeting (GB). An overall expenditure cap that is comprehensive in both demographic scope and medical services coverage.

GNP. See Gross National Product.

Gross Domestic Product (GDP). GNP less foreign market earnings.

Gross National Product (GNP). Total annual value of a nation's goods and services.

HAA. See Health Access America.

HCFA. See Health Care Financing Administration.

Health Access America (HAA). AMA's proposal for ensuring universal health care access.

Health Care Financing Administration (HCFA). Organizational entity within U.S. Department of Health and Human Services that administers Medicare program and the federal portions of Medicaid.

Health Maintenance Organization (HMO). Prepaid group practice, usually covering both hospital and physician services, that contracts to offer an extensive range of health care services in exchange for prospective payment in the form of fixed monthly fees. See box in Chapter 2 for details and varying forms.

HIAA. Health Insurance Association of America

Hill-Burton Act. Hospital Survey and Construction Act of 1946, which provides federal funds for hospital construction.

HMO. See Health Maintenance Organization.

ICU. Intensive Care Unit

Independent Practice Association (IPA). Loose form of HMO in which independently practicing physicians and other providers contract to serve patients within a provider network put together by an insurer; generally without its own facilities.

IPA. See Independent Practice Association.

Living will. Advance directive in which one specifies types and levels of treatment one would or would not want for guidance of family and providers if one later becomes incapable of making needed decisions.

Long-term care (LTC). Nursing-home care.

LTC. See Long-term care.

Managed care. Arrangements with selected providers to deliver care in accord with payer organization guidelines and utilization review; involves insurer supervision of providers beyond simply paying the bills.

Mandated health insurance. Proposals for a legislated requirement that some or all employers offer health insurance coverage for employees.

Medicaid. Joint federal-state public health insurance program for some of the poor, especially those on AFDC, plus pregnant women, children under seven, and nursing-home patients who have largely exhausted their own financial resources.

Medicare. U.S. government health insurance program for persons age 65 and over, for the permanently disabled, and for kidney dialysis treatment. Part A covers hospital expenses; Part B covers fees of physicians and other extrahospital providers.

MIA. Medically Indigent Adult

Moral hazard. Insurance economics term referring to the temptation (= hazard) to overutilize services because a third party is paying for them.

MRI. Magnetic Resonance Imaging

National Health Insurance (NHI). Two meanings in current usage: 1. A publicly
   (i.e., tax)-financed insurance plan to cover the entire population, whether
   financed and operated by the national government or jointly by national
   and state governments. Extension of Medicare to the entire population
   would be an example of an entirely national plan; Canada's system, with
   dual financing from the national government and the governments of the
   provinces, and operation at the provincial level, exemplifies the intergovernmental type. 2. Any health insurance system established by national
   law to cover the entire population but using a mixture of public- and
   private-sector financing and operation. This broader conception is sometimes called Universal Health Insurance (UHI) to indicate the scope of
   coverage without necessarily implying governmental operation. Germany's system is an example, as are the current U.S. play-or-pay proposals.
   Using both terms would make public discussions more precise, with
   universal coverage the policy goal and national plans in the first sense
   being but one means. However, NHI is used at times in both senses, so
   one has to examine the details to see what is really meant.
NFIB. National Federation of Independent Businesses
NHI. See National Health Insurance.

PET. Positron Emission Tomography
Play-or-Pay (PoP). Proposals that would mandate that employers either offer
   health insurance to employees or pay a payroll tax that would be used to
   fund an alternative public plan.
PNHP. Physicians for a National Health Program
PoP. See Play-or-Pay.
PPO. See Preferred Provider Organization.
PPP. Participating Physician Program
PPRC. Physician Payment Review Commission
PPS. See Prospective Payment System.
Practice guidelines. Research-derived criteria for aiding physicians and pa-
   tients in determining appropriate care for specific medical conditions.
   (Also called "protocols" or "practice parameters.")
Preferred provider. Hospital or physician that has contracted with an insurer or
   HMO to provide care on a discounted-charges basis for plan members.
Preferred Provider Organization (PPO). An insurance arrangement that gives
   member patients a higher reimbursement if they go to a provider (who
   will accept a discounted fee) on the PPO's list.
PRO. Professional Review Organization
ProPAC. Prospective Payment Assessment Commission
Prospective Payment System (PPS). Payment arrangements in which the
   amount to be reimbursed by the payer is set before the services are
   performed—by per diem, capitation, or DRG—rather than retrospectively
   on the basis of a fee for each service. Contrasts with FFS.

Relative Value Scale (RVS). A system developed for Medicare that establishes a fee schedule for physician payments on the basis of a score for each service that takes into account the resources used in that service: practice costs, specialized training, and work input that includes time, skill, and judgment required.
RVS. See Relative Value Scale.

Self-insurance. Some employers use their own funds to run their employee-benefit health reimbursement programs rather than buying insurance policies from another organization.
SSI. See Supplementary Security Income.
Stop-loss provision. Insurance arrangement in which patient copayment requirement ceases and insurer covers 100 percent after a certain dollar level of out-of-pocket expense has been reached.
Supplementary Security Income (SSI). Federal income support program for low-income elderly, disabled, and blind persons.

TA. See Technology Assessment.
Technology Assessment (TA). Process of examining newly proposed medical technologies to determine the value of making them widely available, the appropriate conditions for their use, and their insurance reimbursability.
Third-party payment. Payment for health services made by insurance company, employer, or government program rather than by patient.
TPA. Tissue Plasminogen Activator

UHI. See Universal Health Insurance.
Uncompensated care. Services for which hospital receives no payment or payment below cost of providing the service.
Universal Health Insurance (UHI). See National Health Insurance.
UR. See Utilization Review.
Utilization Review (UR). Aspect of managed care in which payer representatives oversee and control use of medical resources by both patient and provider. Includes presurgery second-opinion requirements; prehospital clearance for need and length of stay; gatekeeping (approval of primary-care physician before patient sees a specialist); and limited reimbursement for an approved service option such as nursing-home or home health care.

Volume Performance Standard (VPS). A Medicare program to set an annual cap on total dollar expenditures for physician services.
VPS. See Volume Performance Standard.

Suggested Readings

The literature on health care policy is voluminous, and much of it is rapidly outdated as new ideas, new research findings, and new political approaches arise. Among the books that I think are of continuing interest today for their facts, analyses, and thought-provoking qualities are the following:

Aaron, Henry J., and William B. Schwartz, *The Painful Prescription: Rationing Hospital Care* (Washington, DC: The Brookings Institution, 1984).

Califano, Joseph A., Jr., *America's Health Care Revolution: Who Lives? Who Dies? Who Pays?* (New York: Random House, 1986).

Callahan, Daniel, *Setting Limits: Medical Goals in an Aging Society* (New York: Simon and Schuster, 1987).

Evans, Robert G., *Strained Mercy: The Economics of Canadian Health Care* (Toronto: Butterworths, 1984). (Despite the Canadian context, this is the best single book on the peculiar economics of health care anywhere.)

Fein, Rashi, *Medical Care, Medical Costs: The Search for a Health Insurance Policy* (Cambridge, MA: Harvard University Press, 1986).

Fuchs, Victor R., *Who Shall Live?* (New York: Basic Books, 1974).

Hiatt, Howard H., *America's Health in the Balance: Choice or Chance?* (New York: Harper & Row, 1987).

Payer, Lynn, *Medicine & Culture: Varieties of Treatment in the United States, England, West Germany, and France* (New York: Henry Holt, 1988).

Starr, Paul, *The Social Transformation of American Medicine* (New York: Basic Books, 1982).

Stevens, Rosemary, *In Sickness and in Wealth: American Hospitals in the Twentieth Century* (New York: Basic Books, 1989).

For specific topics, the following are good starting points for further exploration:

On earlier struggles toward national health insurance: Numbers, Ronald L., *Almost Persuaded: American Physicians and Compulsory Health Insurance, 1912–1920* (Johns Hopkins University Press, 1978); Hirshfield, Daniel S., *The Lost Reform: The Campaign for Compulsory Health Insurance in the United States from 1932 to 1943* (Harvard University Press, 1970); Poen, Monty M., *Harry S. Truman Versus the Medical Lobby* (University of Missouri Press, 1979); and Marmor, Theodore R., *The Politics of Medicare* (Chicago: Aldine, 1973).

On the ethics of health care distribution as a matter of social justice: Churchill, Larry R., *Rationing Health Care in America: Perceptions and Principles of Justice* (University of Notre Dame Press, 1987); and Daniels, Norman, *Just Health Care* (New York: Cambridge University Press, 1985).

On the Washington politics of some recent health care policy decisions: Sorian, Richard, *The Bitter Pill: Tough Choices in America's Health Policy* (New York and Washington, DC: McGraw-Hill Healthcare Information Center, 1988).

On recent developments in foreign health care systems: Organization for Economic Cooperation and Development (OECD), *Health Care Systems in Transition* (Paris, 1990); and OECD, *The Reform of Health Systems in Seven Countries* (Paris, 1992).

On the vital and basic, but oft-neglected, role of public health: Institute of Medicine, *The Future of Public Health* (Washington, DC: National Academy Press, 1988).

On all of these topics, as on health care policy generally, periodicals are essential supplements to books. Among those of greatest usefulness, and some public accessibility, are the *New York Times*; the *New England Journal of Medicine*; *Health Affairs*; the *Journal of Health Politics, Policy and Law*; *Business and Health*; *Milbank Quarterly*; the *Journal of the American Medical Association*; and the *Health Care Financing Review*. *National Journal* is a good source for current policy developments, and the *New England Journal* is especially valuable for occasional reports on both foreign health care systems and domestic health care politics by John K. Iglehart, as well as for a continuous stream of thoughtful position papers by physicians and health analysts under the heading "The Sounding Board."

About the Book
and Author

With private health insurance costs averaging over $300 per month, per person—and with 36 million Americans lacking coverage of any sort—it is easy to understand why health care has captured the public imagination as *the* domestic policy issue of the 1990s. Americans spend well over $800 billion a year on health care, yet we are neglecting basic medical attention—like shots and checkups—for our neediest citizens, including over 8 million children.

The American health care "system," if we can call it that, is a costly, bewildering array of acronyms, institutions, people, and procedures that will probably become even more confusing before it gains some clarity. *Curing the Crisis* is the book to read to get a brief but comprehensive picture of the issues—without wading through a lot of technical jargon. In a short, readable, and objective presentation, *Curing the Crisis* offers insight into the following questions:

- What has happened to the availability and cost of health care in recent years, and what are current trends?
- What are the problems with our current health care system, and why do so many Americans lack health insurance despite our spending more per person on health care than any other country?
- What major proposals for health care reform aim at making sure everyone is covered, and what are the pros and cons of each?
- What can we learn from health care systems in Canada, Great Britain, and Germany?
- What are the major proposals for reducing the rate of cost inflation in health care, and how are medical professionals and economists reacting to such plans?

Without advocating any single plan, the author—a scholar and policy specialist—boldly outlines the features he considers essential to a medically, financially, and politically effective cure to the health care system's ailments. In addition to synthesizing and "translating" information from a wide variety of sources, he provides special feature boxes, health care vignettes, a glossary of terms, and case studies from all over the globe for an accessible and engaging presentation. *Curing the Crisis* is appropriate for a variety of readers who want to stay abreast of the issues in American health care that develop in the political arena as well as close to home.

Michael D. Reagan is professor emeritus at the University of California–Riverside and has authored numerous publications on American government and politics including *Regulation: The Politics of Policy, The New Federalism, Science and the Federal Patron, The Managed Economy,* and articles on health care in the *New England Journal of Medicine.*

Index

Aaron, Henry J., 155
Abram, Morris B., 141–142
Access to health care, 39–50,
    57–64, 169–170
Advance directives, 142–144
Aetna Life and Casualty Company,
    47
AFDC. *See* Aid to Families with
    Dependent Children
A. Foster Higgins survey, 48, 124
Agency for Health Care Policy and
    Research (AHCPR), 128, 131,
    133–134
AHCPR. *See* Agency for Health Care
    Policy and Research
AIDS, 66
Aid to Families with Dependent
    Children (AFDC), 42
Allied Signal Corporation, 47
Alternative Delivery Systems
    (ADS), 17, 135
American Academy of Family
    Physicians Foundation, 140
American Academy of Pediatrics,
    43
American College of Physicians,
    128
American Hospital Association, 29,
    121, 195
American Medical Association, 7,
    32, 84, 96, 105–106
American Nurses Association, 168
Americare plan, 99

An American Approach, 101–103
Artificial heart, 23, 71

BCBSA. *See* Blue Cross and Blue
    Shield Association
Bentsen, Lloyd, 108
Blue Cross, 29, 49
Blue Cross and Blue Shield
    Association (BCBSA), 105, 107,
    132
Blue Shield, 30, 49
Brook, Robert H., 70, 130
Brown, Lawrence D., 19
Bush, George, 106
Business and Health survey, 47
Butler, Stuart M., 108

California's durable power form,
    143–144
Callahan, Daniel, 155
Canada's health care, 53, 85–86,
    88–92, 102, 149–150, 169
Caper, Philip, 131
Caronna, John, 69
Carter, Jimmy, 168
Case management, 122–123
CAT-scans, 67–68
Certificate-of-Need (CON), 154
Chafee, John H., 106
CHAMPUS. *See* Civilian Health and
    Medical Program of the Armed
    Forces

CHC. *See* Community Health Centers
Children's Medicaid Coalition, 177
Chrysler Corporation, 52
Civilian Health and Medical Program of the Armed Forces (CHAMPUS), 133
Clinical guidelines. *See* Practice guidelines
COBRA program, 33
Cohen, Harvey J., 72
Community Health Centers (CHC), 14
Competition, 61–64, 99–108, 117–119
CON. *See* Certificate-of-Need
Copayments, 60
Corporatism, 95, 151
Cost-containment efforts, 26, 32–33, 62–64, 111–159
   capacity constraints, 147–155
   economic model, 113–126
   medical model, 126–137, 144–147
   overall controls, 139–159
   partial controls, 111–138
   role of patients, 139–144
Cost-effectiveness, 68, 113, 133–134
Cost-sharing, 61, 95–96, 114–117, 169–170
Cost-shifting, 35, 63, 115, 121
Cross subsidies, 34–35
Culture of medicine, 22–23, 72, 144–147

Defensive medicine, 75–76, 119
Diagnostic Related Groups (DRGs), 24, 119–120, 154
DRGs. *See* Diagnostic Related Groups

Durable power of attorney for health affairs, 142–144

Economics of health care, 57–64, 72–77, 99–101, 111–112
Economists, views of, 5–6
Eddy, David M., 127
Ellwood, Paul M., 128
Enthoven, Alain C., 99, 166
EPOs. *See* Exclusive provider organizations
Evans, Robert G., 74, 90
Exclusive provider organizations (EPOs), 18–19

FDA. *See* Food and Drug Administration, U.S.
Feder, Judith M., 78
Federalism, 21, 89, 149, 171–172
Fee-for-service (FFS) payment, 77–78
FFS. *See* Fee-for-service payment
Financial Accounting Standards Board, 61, 112
Financial incentives, 23–27, 73–78
First-dollar coverage, 47
Food and Drug Administration, U.S. (FDA), 50
Ford, Gerald R., 168
Ford Motor Company, 52
Free Rider problem, 170

General Electric Corporation, 112
General Motors Corporation (GM), 48, 112
Germany's health care, 94–96, 150–151
Ginzberg, Eli, 159
Global budgeting, 78–80, 147–155
GM. *See* General Motors Corporation

Great Britain's health care, 3, 53,
    85–88, 145

Harvard Community Health Plan,
    140
Hatch, Orrin G., 71
HCFA. *See* Health Care Financing
    Administration
Health Access America (HAA),
    105–106, 168
Health care
    costs, 16, 50–54, 64–70, 77. *See
    also* Cost-containment efforts
    economic characteristics, 57–64
    as an industry, 65, 71
Health Care Financing
    Administration (HCFA), 8,
    133–134
Health insurance
    and access to care, 57–64
    administrative costs of, 67, 92
    community rating, 49
    and employment, 46–50, 61,
        97–106, 112
    experience rating, 49, 62
    mandate approach to, 103–106
    market approach to, 57–64
    occupational blacklisting, 49
    play-or-pay approach to, 97–103
    public sector approaches,
        85–103, 168–169
    reforms in private insurance,
        106–109
    See also Uninsured
Health Insurance Association of
    America (HIAA), 105, 107,
    121–122
Health maintenance organizations
    (HMOs), 17–19, 25–26, 100,
    124, 154, 166
Henderson, Donald A., 54

Heritage Foundation, 108–109
HIAA. *See* Health Insurance
    Association of America
High-technology medicine, 67–72
Hill-Burton Act, 30
HMOs. *See* Health maintenance
    organizations
Holahan, John, 101
Hospices, 137
Hospitals, 24, 27–31, 34–35, 76,
    119

ICU. *See* Intensive Care Unit
Ideology, 83–85, 90–91
Imaging technology, 67–69
Immunization, 10, 54
Independent Practice Associations
    (IPAs), 18
Indian Health Service, 14
Infant mortality, 9, 53
Insurance. *See* Health insurance
Intensive Care Unit (ICU),
    154–155
IPAs. *See* Independent Practice
    Associations

Japan, 53
Johnson, Lyndon B., 32

Kaiser Permanente, 18, 120
Kennedy, Edward M., 71, 99, 104
Kerry, Bob, 94
Kimball, Justin Ford, 28–29

Leaf, Alexander, 146
Life expectancy, 9, 153
Life-style behavior, 139–141
Living will, 142
Long-term care (LTC), 45, 170
Lowe, Morton, 90

LTC. *See* Long-term Care

McClure, Walter, 117
Magnetic Resonance Imaging
    (MRI), 67–69
Malpractice, 75–78, 118–119
Managed care, 121–126
Managed competition, 99–101
Mandate approach, 103–106
Measles, 10, 54
Medicaid, 6, 20–21, 32, 42–45, 52,
    64, 121, 157–158, 170–171,
    176
Medically Indigent Adults, 42
Medicare, 21, 24, 26–27, 32, 44–46,
    52, 113, 119–121, 134, 157,
    165
Mitchell, George J., 99
Moral hazard, 72–77
MRI. *See* Magnetic Resonance
    Imaging

NAM. *See* National Association of
    Manufacturers
Nancy Cruzan court case, 144
National Association of
    Manufacturers (NAM), 47, 54
National Association of
    Wholesaler-Distributors, 54
National Federation of
    Independent Businesses
    (NFIB), 52, 54
National Health Insurance (NHI),
    31–32, 85–86, 88–94
National Health Service, 86–88
National Health Service Corps, 14,
    106
National Heart, Lung and Blood
    Institute, 71
National Institutes of Health, 5,
    128, 135

National Leadership Coalition for
    Health Care Reform, 168
NFIB. *See* National Federation of
    Independent Businesses
NHI. *See* National Health Insurance
Nixon, Richard M., 104
NPs. *See* Nurse practitioners
Nurse practitioners (NPs), 136
Nurses, 65, 71
Nursing homes, 45

Oregon rationing plan, 157–158
Out-of-pocket expenses, 45, 115

Partnership on Health Care and
    Employment, 168
PAs. *See* Physician assistants
Patients, roles of, 73–77, 116–117,
    139–147
Patient Self-Determination Act,
    144
Payer, Lynn, 145
PET. *See* Positron Emission
    Tomography
Physician assistants (PAs), 136
Physician
    autonomy, 7, 152, 173–174
    fees, 26–27. *See also* Relative
        Value Scale; Volume
        Performance Standard
    incomes, 65
Physician Payment Review
    Commission (PPRC), 151–152
Physicians for a National Health
    Plan (PNHP) 166
Play-or-pay (PoP), 97–103,
    167–168
Pluralism, 174–175
PNHP. *See* Physicians for a National
    Health Program
Politics of health care, 164–166

PoP. *See* Play-or-pay
Positron Emission Tomography
    (PET), 67–69
PPOs. *See* Preferred Provider
    Organizations
PPRC. *See* Physician Payment
    Review Commission
PPS. *See* Prospective payment
    system
Practice
    guidelines, 127–131
    variations, 127
Preferred Provider Organizations
    (PPOs), 18–19
Prescription drugs, 50, 53
Prevention, 9, 137, 140
Private collectivism, 60
Procedural medicine, 70–71
Professional Review Organizations,
    121
ProPAC. *See* Prospective Payment
    Advisory Commission
Prospective Payment Advisory
    Commission (ProPAC),
    151–152
Prospective payment system (PPS),
    24, 119–121
Protocols. *See* Practice, guidelines
Prudent buyer approach, 117
Prudential Insurance Company,
    123
Public Health Service, 133
Public opinion, 54, 164–165

Queuing, 87–88, 153, 158

RAND, 61, 115, 127–128
Rationing, 155–158
Reagan Administration, 43
Regionalization, 136
Reinhardt, Uwe, 3, 111

Relative Value Scale (RVS), 26, 120
Robert Wood Johnson Foundation
    survey, 55
Rockefeller, John D., IV, 98, 99
Rockefeller-Pepper Commission
    Plan, 98–99, 166
Roosevelt, Franklin D., 32
Rostenkowski, Dan, 108
Ross, Judith Wilson, 145
RVS. *See* Relative Value Scale

Schramm, Carl J., 107
Schwartz, Mike, 71
Schwartz, William B., 132, 155
Self-insurance, 63
Socialism, 84
Socialized medicine, 83–85
Southern California Edison, 47,
    123
SSI. *See* Supplemental Security
    Income
State-government roles, 42–45,
    97–103, 157–158, 168–169,
    171–172
Sullivan, Louis W., 139, 140
Supplemental Security Income
    (SSI), 42

TA. *See* Technology assessment
Tax subsidies for health care, 115,
    168–169
Technology, 32, 54, 67–72
Technology assessment (TA),
    131–135
Third-party payment, 15, 73–77
Tissue Plasminogen Activator
    (TPA), 69–70
Todd, James S., 7
TPA. *See* Tissue Plasminogen
    Activator
Truman, Harry S., 32, 84

UHI. *See* Universal health
 insurance
Uncompensated care, 35
Uninsured, 6, 15, 39–41
United States Congress, 4, 166
Universal health insurance (UHI),
 85–86, 94–103
Universalism, 169
UR. *See* Utilization Review
Urban Institute, The, 101
U.S. Bipartisan (Pepper)
 Commission on
 Comprehensive Health Care,
 98–99

U.S. Chamber of Commerce, 54
Utilization review (UR), 77,
 122–125

Vladeck, Bruce C., 21
Volume Performance Standard
 (VPS), 27, 120, 151
VPS. *See* Volume Performance
 Standard

Weber, Carl, 3
Wennberg, John E., 127
Wofford, Harris, 10